Margaret Vandegrift

Holidays at Home

Margaret Vandegrift

Holidays at Home

ISBN/EAN: 9783337289881

Printed in Europe, USA, Canada, Australia, Japan

Cover: Foto ©ninafisch / pixelio.de

More available books at **www.hansebooks.com**

"MOPSY WATCHED THE SPARROWS HOLDING HIGH FESTIVAL OVER HIS BREAKFAST."
Frontispiece. See Page 144.

Holidays at Home:

FOR

Boys and Girls.

By Margaret Vandegrift,

Author of "Clover Beach" and "Under the Dog-Star."

Porter & Coates,
Philadelphia.

CONTENTS.

	PAGE
THE THREE PHILOSOPHERS	9
THE COURAGEOUS HARE	14
MINCE AND STEW	17
WHAT PEPPER SAID	28
THE OLD PILOT	32
THE ILL-BRED DUCKS	35
A TRUE KNIGHT	40
"IN A MINUTE"	55
THE TRAVELS OF A CHRISTMAS TREE	65
HOME WITH THE TIDE	81
COURAGE	84
A HAPPY BIRTHDAY	98
THE KING'S THREE SONS	115
TWO GOOD FRIENDS	124
TWO WAYS	144
THE MAY-QUEEN	159
MRS. CLUCK'S CHILDREN	163

CONTENTS.

	PAGE
DARING	174
THE END OF THE RAINBOW	197
A COUNTRY MONTH	202
OLD NURSE	228
FATHER CHRISTMAS	233
THE BABES IN THE WOOD	241
A MAYFLOWER	251
AN OLD-FASHIONED FATHER	256
A HOT SUPPER	261
ONE STEP AT A TIME	266
THE THREE B'S	272
MAKING A TABLEAU	280
A YOUNG EGYPTIAN	288
UNCLE MOSES	291
A GENEROUS DOG	296

ILLUSTRATIONS.

	PAGE
"Mopsy watched the sparrows holding high festival over his breakfast"	Frontispiece.
"Mince was playing happily with a large ball"	19
"He gave it a vigorous stroke with his paw"	23
"He was putting the last touches to a little vessel"	25
"Well, row the bonny maidens"	33
"She turned her back on him and sat down in the grass"	37
"A beautiful rainbow spanned the pond"	47
"Grandma sent Bijou with a bunch of grapes"	49
"Two refractory horses objected to being shod"	52
The donkeys of Ruth's dream	59
"She seated one of the dolls on her lap"	61
"Rena once more counted the money in her hand"	67
"Happy little children woke to search their stockings"	75
"She sat on a rock and waited"	82
"Lion was already pulling Baby May from the water"	93
"Rover and Douglas and the cat and the kitten watched her"	105
"Each of my subjects must sing at least once a day"	117
Deer in the forest	121
"The baby waked and played with his fingers"	131
"Clementine was asleep"	139
"Almost under his feet was a snipe"	141
"Polly liked ironing, ... and she did it with all her might"	147
"Puck, the cat, was walking round Prince's watering-trough"	153
"The baby, seated on a stool, and Mopsy, in a chair, each sang"	157
"Sceptre and train to grace your queen"	160
"Seek for your queen where hidden lie"	161
"The professor of crowing gave them an hour's lesson"	167
"Little waterfalls came bursting out between the staves"	171

ILLUSTRATIONS.

	PAGE
"She fed Don from her hand for the last time"	175
"We've been talking over the wall"	179
"They found her standing in the cove beside the old pier"	183
"A little basket, filled with a cat-bird's nest, swung from a bough"	187
"A boy by the wayside bravely seized the bridle and held him"	193
"She was lying there, the darling!"	200
"That lovely bath in the water-butt was too cold for her"	203
"Cecil fed the cows out of his hand"	209
"Joe was whittling out a willow whistle for Cecil"	221
"Two fawns, then the doe, and then the stag"	224
"A frog had fallen into the clutches of a white goose"	227
"Sometimes she tells of the 'good folks'"	231
"Grandpa stood there . . . with Polly's wreath on his head"	235
"Fred can cut out animals very nicely"	239
"As the sparrow went peeping about he met a horned beetle"	243
"There the sparrow found them next morning, asleep"	247
"Nothing more she knew until, to a burst of music"	253
Mr. Bullfrog teaching his youngsters to swim	257
"Five young sparrows saw it, and each made a dart for it"	263
"She turned aside to a furze-bank, and wearily sat down"	267
"He pipes for my dolly's dancing"	270
Jet and Pearl and the Calf	275
"Aunt Alice stood me on a chair before a little girl"	281
"They stopped me in the middle of a game of Blindman's Buff"	285
"What a very solemn-looking little boy!"	289
"When he is not smoking . . . he tells made-up stories"	293
"Reginald gave Dot a gentle throw into a wave"	301

Holidays at Home.

THE THREE PHILOSOPHERS.

THE cow had lived there always; at least she supposed she had, for she could not remember any other home, and she had a sort of misty recollection of trotting about that very barnyard with her mother when her legs were not good for much. So she felt it her duty to be polite to the cock and the turkey, who were comparatively new-comers.

The cock came first. He came in a basket, and a very uncomfortable time he had of it; the basket was too small for him; it doubled up his neck and made his back ache. But it didn't take the crow out of him. He gave a good loud "Cock-a-doodle-doo-oo-oo!"

two or three times as the farm-wagon jolted over the frozen road; he wished to let the farmer know that he was merely suppressed, not conquered; and he had his reward. The farmer set the basket down on the out-kitchen floor and called his wife.

"Come here, Sally," he said, "and see what a fine fellow I've brought you: he's crowed me all the way home. I'll warrant *he'll* not steal the corn and worms from the hens."

The farmer had unfastened the basket while he was talking, and the cock stepped proudly out with the loudest crow he had given yet. He was introduced to the chicken-yard at once, and was very careful to act up to the good character which had been given him.

Not many days after the turkey-gobbler came, and it was in comparing notes about their journey that he and the cock became such great friends. The turkey had come on horseback, with his legs tied together; he had ridden in front of the farmer, and he had not liked it. The cow was very kind to both of them. She was older than they were, and she gave them a great deal of good advice, but they did not mind it much.

"You see, we can always *take* it pleasantly," said the cock to the turkey confidentially; "that will please her, you know, and we are not bound to *follow* it. She's a good old thing, but she's never been either a turkey or a cock—at least I don't believe she has; she has no recollection of it."

What the cow chiefly advised them about was being philosophical.

"Don't fret, don't worry, don't excite yourselves," she would say,

"'Fair and easy goes far in a day.' It's best to take life calmly and coolly."

"That's pretty good doctrine for a cow, perhaps," the cock would say to the turkey, "but I don't think the hens would think much of it, especially when grub-time comes."

The farmer drove into the yard one day with a fine load of cabbages from a distant field; his little boy sat on the high seat in front of the wagon, holding the reins.

"Oh, father," he cried, "mayn't I throw this small cabbage to Crumple? She looks as if she wanted one so."

"Throw away, then," said the farmer, good-naturedly; and the little boy threw, but not hard enough; the cabbage fell on the wrong

"JUST THEN THE COCK AND THE TURKEY SAUNTERED UP."

side of the trough, where Crumple could not possibly reach it. Just then the dinner-horn was blown, and the boy, never stopping to look which way the cabbage went, jumped down and ran into the house. Crumple was very much annoyed at first, but just then the cock and the turkey sauntered up, and it occurred to her that here was a fine chance to show them how philosophical she was. So she told them, in a pleasant conversational manner, what had happened, but expressed no wish for the cabbage nor anger at the boy.

The cock and the turkey, however, were quite indignant at the boy, and said that if he couldn't throw straighter than that he'd better not have thrown at all.

"Don't get so excited," said the cow mildly; "you see how calmly I am taking it."

"It strikes me that you're taking it more calmly than there's any sense in," said the cock, a little irritably.—"See here, friend Turkey, if you'll take a good grip of one of those thick stems with your bill, I'll take another, and then, if we both lift together, and Mrs. Crumple will just stretch as far over the trough as she can, she shall have her cabbage, after all."

To this Mrs. Crumple, after many apologies for the trouble she was giving, consented; and when the boy came out from dinner she was munching the cabbage with much satisfaction.

"I'd like to know how in the world that cow managed to reach that cabbage," said the farmer; "I saw it fall outside the trough."

"Well, ma'am," said the cock as Crumple took the last mouthful. "don't you like our philosophy rather better than your own?"

"Perhaps it is better," said the cow reluctantly—she did not like to yield a principle—"but I'm quite willing to admit that four heads are better than two, if one *is* a cabbage-head."

THE COURAGEOUS HARE.

THE hare lay down on the bank of a stream, weak and weary with running. She had succeeded in escaping the hounds, but she felt that a few more runs such as that which she had made this morning would cost her her life.

"I might as well let the hounds kill me and be done with it," she murmured sadly to herself, "if I am to die of fright or of heart disease."

Just then a frog hopped upon the bank, close by her head.

"Oh, how you made me jump!" she exclaimed. "Couldn't you possibly learn to walk, instead of hopping in that startling manner?"

"I'm very sorry," said the frog humbly. "I didn't mean to startle you, I'm sure, but it's the only way I can go; it's the way my legs are made, you know. But what has happened? You look dreadfully used up."

"Those dreadful hounds have been after me again," groaned the hare. "And I've three quarters of a mind just to drown myself and put an end to it. They'll catch me some day, and I'd rather be drowned than eaten—wouldn't you?"

"Well, of course *I* would," said the frog, "because when they thought I was drowned I wouldn't be; but if you'll excuse me for seeming to dictate to a warm-blooded animal, and one so much larger than myself, I'll tell you what I've been resolving this morning. The boys in this neighborhood are as eager for my blood as the hounds are for yours—I heard some of them once saying my hind legs tasted just like pork, the cannibals!—and though I've always succeeded in getting off so far, they may surround me and catch me any day; so I've made up my mind what to do. I heard one of the little wretches tell how he got away from an angry bull that was chasing him. 'I looked him right square in the eye,' he said, 'and backed slowly off to the fence; and he actually stood still and didn't follow me.' Now, I'm going to try that the very next time they chase me. I shall just look steadily at them and back off, and they'll not dare to follow me. If you'd like to try it, we might practise on each other, you know, so as to learn to look a good while without winking—it might spoil it to wink, I suppose—and then the next time we are chased let's just stand up firmly and unflinchingly, and back off at our leisure."

"You really are very intelligent for so small an animal," said the hare, admiringly. "We'll begin at once; it will quiet my nerves, and there's no telling how soon we may need to try it."

So for fully five minutes the hare and frog silently and steadily looked each other in the eyes without flinching.

A large spider had been concealed under a blackberry-leaf

directly over the hare's head, and now he chuckled to himself: "I'll give them a chance to try their courage on something small, just to get their hands in, as it were."

So he softly let himself down by some of the string which he always carried in his pocket, and tickled the hare's nose. She was so busy looking the frog in the eyes that she felt him before she saw him, and, lifting her eyes suddenly, she mistook his dark body for a dog on the other side of the stream. With a terrified squeal, and forgetting her fatigue at once, she bounded into the bushes, and never stopped until she was a mile away, while the frog, without stopping to see what had frightened her, plunged into the water.

The spider drew himself up to the blackberry-bough, chuckling harder than ever. "My grandmother was quite right," he said to himself: "'Brag's a good dog, but Holdfast is a better.'"

MINCE AND STEW.

IF you had asked Mrs. Ahashuerus—who was a large gray-and-black cat with a severe expression of countenance—where she lived, she would have said, "In the very best cat boarding-house that ever was kept. They give us fish nearly all the time; they keep the house afloat a long way from land, so that neither boys nor dogs have a chance at us; and they have put up a gymnasium in the upper story, expressly that I may teach my kittens how to climb."

This was *her* view of it. The real fact was, that she and her children, and until his sudden death her husband, lived on board a trim little sailing vessel engaged in the coast-trade, and that as every one, from the cook and the captain bold down to the midshipmite, liked cats, and especially kittens, she was allowed to believe that the whole establishment was kept up expressly for her benefit.

She had met with one great sorrow since she came on board in the loss of her husband; otherwise, her life had been one of unclouded sunshine. Mr. Ahashuerus, who was a bold and daring cat, had been named by the captain, who was fond of ancient history, and his wife of course was called Mrs. Ahashuerus, but, as the sailors had a good deal to do, the name was shortened to Hash; and when the two kittens were born, the mate, who had asked the privilege of naming them, called them Mince and Stew. It was shortly after this that the head of the family, recklessly climbing the rigging one dark night, was pitched into the sea by a sudden lurch of the vessel, and went down before a line could be cast out to save him. His wife, who had been called indifferently "Mrs. Hash" and "The Missus," was now generally called simply Hash. She brooded over her loss a good deal; for, although Mr. Ahashuerus had not been a model husband, having been somewhat uncertain as to his temper, she thought, now that he was gone, that he had been a good deal better than nobody; she missed the companionship of some one of her own age, and she foresaw trouble in bringing up Stew: he was wilful and impertinent, and had a particular fancy for doing whatever he was told not do and going wherever he knew he had better not go. Mince, on the contrary, was gentle and obedient. She was a great favorite with the captain, while Stew, who knew well enough "on which side of his butter to look for his bread," had, by sundry blandishments and exceptional good behavior when he was in the galley, made the cook his firm friend. "*He's* a cat

"MINCE WAS PLAYING HAPPILY WITH A LARGE BALL." See Page 21.

with some spirit to him," the cook would say; "and he's a good, sensible dark color, that don't show every little smudge."

Hash always felt uneasy when the vessel was in port: boys and dogs had once or twice come on board, and she was afraid, too, that the kittens might stray along the gangplank and be lost on that great unknown world, the shore. So one day, when the vessel was moored for a few hours to a particularly noisy wharf, upon which she had seen several dogs running about, she called the kittens into the captain's state-room, and told them it would be safer for all three to stay quietly there until the vessel should sail again, which, she had heard the captain say, would be late that afternoon, at the turn of the tide. The captain had very kindly made a bed for Hash and her family in the snug enclosed place under his berth, and Stew crawled sulkily into this bed, saying that if they were to stay all day in that stupid place, he might as well go to sleep. Mince was playing happily with a large ball which one of the sailors had brought the kittens that morning, and which bounced delightfully. Stew was watching her, and wishing he had not said he would go to sleep, and Hash, with her eyes cast thoughtfully on the floor, was musing on the different dispositions of her children, and wishing Stew were more like Mince, when the captain's voice was suddenly heard, calling, "Hash! Hash!" loudly and excitedly.

Hash never disobeyed her captain, so she sprang up, stopping only to say to the children, "Stay here until I come back."

Then she ran to the place from which the captain's voice seemed to come. He was in the hold.

"There's a whopping big rat behind this box, old lady," he said as soon as Hash appeared. "Steady now! be ready for it as I move the box."

Hash was ready, and succeeded in grasping the rat by the neck, but he turned and gave her such a ferocious bite that with a howl of pain she dropped him, and he scuttled behind a larger box. Then began an exciting chase: the captain was obliged to call the midshipmite to help corner the rat, which was finally caught and killed, but not before the action had lasted nearly half an hour.

Meanwhile, Mince had grown tired of playing ball by herself, and had vainly begged Stew to join her. "You see," she said, "if you'd sit over there while I sit here, we could roll it back and forth beautifully; it's a very rolly sort of ball."

"That's stupid," answered Stew fretfully, "and besides, I'm hungry—hungrier than I've been for weeks—and I'm sure mamma has forgotten us; she couldn't have meant us to go without our dinners. And it's perfectly safe in the galley—just as safe as it is here, and safer—for cook would take care of us if anything were to come on board; and I should just like to know what we would do, all by ourselves, if anything were to come in here. Come on; I *must* have something to eat right away, this minute."

Mince was a timid little thing—Stew frequently called her a "'fraid cat"—and after Stew's unpleasant suggestions she did not dare to be left alone; so, very unwillingly, and with the feeling that she was doing wrong, she followed Stew into the galley, which, you know, is the ship's kitchen. Nobody was there, but a large basket, with a cover laid loosely upon it, stood near the table; it was full of something moving, and all around the edge stuck out queer-looking claws. Mince immediately jumped on the table to be out of harm's way, and to examine this strange basketful at her leisure; but Stew's curiosity was more active.

"HE GAVE IT A VIGOROUS STROKE WITH HIS PAW."

"I think they're some new kind of mice," he said excitedly. "And how proud mamma would be if I were to catch one! I mean to see if I can."

"You'd better let them alone," said Mince fearfully; "they look dreadfully wicked, to me."

"Baby!" said Stew disdainfully; and, giving a spring and a grab all at once, he succeeded in pulling out on the floor one of the curious creatures, which, as you have probably guessed, were lobsters.

He stood staring at it for a moment, rather frightened at the result of his daring, but instead of trying to get away, it lay quite still, excepting a feeble motion of its claws.

"Stupid thing! why don't it run?" said Stew impatiently. "I'll see if I can't make it." And he gave it a vigorous poke with his paw.

Alas, poor Stew! The lobster fastened on his soft little paw with an iron grip, and all his frantic shaking and shrieking failed to make it let go. "He'll kill me!" he screamed.—"Oh, Mince, you coward, why don't you come pull him off?"

"I'm afraid," sobbed Mince; "he would grab me; and, besides, you shouldn't have meddled with him, Stew."

Just then the lobster gave an extra hard nip, and Stew dashed out of the door, and, not knowing where he went, up the gang-plank to the wharf, and almost into the arms of—oh, dreadful!—a boy!

He was very busy putting the last touches to a little ship which he had been rigging, and he never looked up, or saw Stew at all, until the lobster struck his bare foot; then he jumped up, nearly as frightened as Stew was. But he soon saw what was the matter, and at first he only laughed, but when he found the poor little kitten was really suffering, and frightened nearly to death besides, he gently held him fast with one hand while with the blade of his large knife he pried open the lobster's claw and set him free.

"I do believe," he said, as he stroked his soft fur and tried to

"HE WAS PUTTING THE LAST TOUCHES TO A LITTLE VESSEL."

See Page 24.

comfort and quiet him, "that you are one of the two kittens that I saw on the deck of that ship this morning. Come, then, I will take you home, poor little thing!" and he carried Stew down the gangplank, holding the lobster carefully in his other hand. The captain and Hash were just coming up out of the hold with the rat, which had at last been caught, and the captain laughed heartily when he heard of Stew's adventure.

"Served him just right," he said; "he's the most meddlesome kitten I ever saw.—And you brought back the lobster, eh, my fine little fellow? Keep it, keep it, and here are a couple more to go with it; take them home for your supper."

Stew was so ashamed that he limped away to bed, and never came out again until the vessel had left port. His mother would have spanked him for his disobedience, but the lame paw hurt him so badly that Hash said it was punishment enough. And indeed it seemed to be, for he gradually broke himself of his dreadful habit of touching everything he came near from that time, and his mother no longer was obliged to tell him a dozen times a day, "Your eyes are not in the ends of your paws, Stew."

WHAT PEPPER SAID.

PEPPER was the dog, "and a good dog too." You had only to look into his eyes to see what a good watch-dog he was; he seemed to look forty ways at once. And no dog ever had so many different barks. There was the roar with which he scared away tramps and chicken-thieves; the pleasant sort of chuckle which he gave when he was told he might follow the wagon; the shout of delight with which he welcomed the children home from school or from a visit; and his talking bark, in which the children declared they could distinguish words.

Fritz and little Irma had just begun to go to school, and Pepper did not like it at all. He missed them dreadfully, and every morning he walked with them to the end of the lane, telling them, as they declared, how sorry he was to have them go and how he could not play without them. But they liked school pretty well, and always told Pepper all about what had happened when they came home. He met them always at the end of the lane as soon as he

"IRMA AND PEPPER SAT ON THE UPPER STEP."

found out when to look for them, and they used to keep some scraps for him in their dinner-basket. But one day the procession came up the lane very silently and solemnly, and Fritz carried his slate as well as his books and the dinner-basket; and when the mother asked what was the matter, Fritz hung his head and answered, "I drew pictures instead of doing my examples, and the master made me bring them home to do; and he told me to ask you not to let me play until they were done. There are three, and they are hard."

"Sit down at once, then, and go to work," said the mother briskly; "they will not grow easier by keeping."

So Fritz took his slate and sat down on the lower doorstep, while little Irma and Pepper sat on the upper one to encourage him.

"We will not play," said Irma, "until you can come and play too."

Pepper had brought the last plaything they had made him—a bunch of long cock's feathers fastened tightly into a large cork—and laid it at Fritz's feet; but when he found there was work on hand, he paid no attention to it, but sat stiffly up on the step—"trying to look like the master," Irma said.

Fritz did not feel like doing sums. He leaned his head on his slate with a great yawn. "If I might play a while first, I should not mind so much," he said fretfully, "but this is like having school all day."

Now, if Pepper did not understand all about it, I should like to know why he broke out that moment with his talking bark. This was what Fritz thought he said: "Go to work and do it! go to work and *do* it! Folks take the time to complain that would do the work. Go to work and do-oo-oo-oo it!"

WHAT PEPPER SAID. 31

"So I will, then," cried Fritz resolutely.

And in just half an hour, by the eight-day clock, the examples were done and the children and Pepper were free to play.

"Oh, my dear Pepper, what a wise dog you are!" said Irma, giving Pepper a hug and a little kiss where his front hair was parted.

And Pepper said, "Thank you."

At least, Irma said he did.

THE OLD PILOT.

O N the frowning height of Wolfsberg a
goodly castle towers
Far, far above the grassy plain, gay with
its summer flowers:
Long had the Kolbergs held it, but now
the time had come
When a stranger knight was threaten-
ing the dear ancestral home.

The land-side was beleaguered. "Our
hope, if hope there be,"
Said the last Kolberg, "resteth in those
beyond the sea.
Ten thousand times 'twere easier a hero's death to die
Than here, like wild beasts caught in snares, helpless and sad to lie."

Old Nettleback the pilot, the oldest man within
The fortress, said, "My master, thy faithlessness is sin ;
For see across the water, as thou speakest thus in grief,
The good ship onward speeding that bringeth us relief."

"WELL ROW THE BONNY MAIDENS."

Then rose a mighty tempest, loudly the whirlwind roared,
The lurid lightning flashing, while hail and rain down poured.
The brave ship struggles onward, the roadway gains at last,
And, as the guns salute her, she lies at anchor fast.

She signals for a pilot, for rocks the channel bound;
Old Nettleback springs forward, but where can men be found?

Not one of that small garrison, who has its perils shared,
Can even for an hour from the defence be spared.

Then cries the pilot cheerily, "Nay, here are maidens stout,
And each one good at rowing.—Come, what are you about?
Dorothy, Frida, Lena, Irmengarde, and Frinette,
Come, take your oars and follow; we'll save the fortress yet!"

Well row the bonny maidens; each arm with hope gains strength;
The pilot's line has fallen across the deck at length.
He gains the ship, and over the ocean's deafening swell
His voice clangs like a trumpet, with the ringing buoy-bell.

" Victory!" yells the garrison; "the ship has gained the shore!"
Their shout of triumph rises above the tempest's roar.
" Now God be praised for courage so strong and sure to win!
We'll gain the day—to doubt it were surely now a sin."

From the German of Feder von Koppen.

THE ILL-BRED DUCKS.

A FAMILY of kingfishers had lived for many years in a wood near a lonely lake. The fishing was good, travellers or sportsmen seldom came that way, and so every spring the old nests were repaired and new ones built in neighboring trees, until the colony was a very large one. But one day came a great excitement. A young kingfisher, who liked to see what was going on, flew home to dinner nearly breathless, and reported that men were building a house near one end of their lake.

"I'm afraid we'll have to move," said the great-grandfather sadly. "If there are men, there are probably boys and guns; we shall be safe no longer."

"But perhaps," said the young kingfisher who had brought the news, hopefully, "they will only shoot our enemies, the hawks, who, if what I am told is true, catch chickens whenever they have a chance, and ducks too. These people have both, and the ducks have already taken possession of one end of our lake."

"That will do no harm," said the great-grandfather; "in fact, it may do good. If those ducks are friendly, we can form an alliance with them; we can agree to warn them when hawks are about, for we have a much better opportunity of seeing them than creatures which do not fly can possibly have; and they can warn us if they see the people in the house making any preparations for gunning. But there is time enough; we will let the people finish their house before we take any active steps, for while they are busy at that I think we shall be quite safe."

Not many weeks passed before the house was completed, and the barn too; then the wife and daughter of the man who had been building them came, and the family settled contentedly in its new home. Now, it was agreed that the young kingfisher who had first brought news of the arrival should make a formal call upon the ducks, and, should they seem friendly, propose the agreement to them.

So he set off, and was pleased to find them gathered together at one end of the pond; the old ducks were looking after some young ones who were taking their first swimming-lesson. He perched upon a bough which overhung the water, and made a few polite remarks about the weather to an old duck who was standing on the bank. She deliberately turned her back to him and sat down in the grass. "Perhaps our language isn't the same," he thought to himself; but just then another duck turned her head slightly toward the first one, and said in a low tone, "Such presumption!"

"SHE TURNED HER BACK ON HIM AND SAT DOWN IN THE GRASS."

The young kingfisher, whose family seldom used a long word when a short one would do as well, did not quite know what "presumption" meant, but he quite understood what it meant when two of the ducklings swam under the stick upon which he was perched, stared very hard at him for a minute, and then swam toward the bank, giggling to each other, "Well, of all the queer-looking creatures!"

"Did you ever see such a bill?"

"And *did* you notice his feet?"

"Impudent thing! trying to scrape acquaintance with *our* family!"

The kingfisher, full of indignation, waited no longer, but flew back to his family and reported how he had been received.

"There is no help for it, then," said the great-grandfather sorrowfully; "we must fly away and found a new colony in that great wood by the river, two days' flight from here."

So the kingfishers sadly left their old home, and founded a new one many miles away.

And a year after the young kingfisher, hovering near the old place to see what changes had been made, heard the man who had built the house saying to a neighbor, "There's no use in trying to keep chickens here, or ducks either; we've had so many carried off by hawks that we've given it up."

A TRUE KNIGHT.

"H, mamma, the funniest old woman you ever saw in your life!" exclaimed little Ernest Kennedy, bursting into his mother's room almost as noisily as if he had been a bombshell, and quite forgetting that his cap was on his head instead of in his hand. But, somehow, something in his mother's smile must have made him remember it, for he turned even a little more red in the face than he had made himself by running, and took off his cap, saying in a much quieter voice, "I beg your pardon, mamma; I didn't think. But I really wish you could have seen her; I never saw anybody that looked at all like her."

"Indeed?" said mamma. "Had she four hands or two heads, or was she a giantess or a dwarf?"

"No: it wasn't in *that* way that she was funny," said Ernest, hesitating a little. "She had on queer shoes that looked like boats, and a sort of fly-away cap instead of a bonnet, and the waist of her dress was 'most up to her neck, and the skirt was so short that it made her look very funny indeed."

"Then it was only her clothing which was 'funny'? said Mrs. Kennedy. "You gave me to understand that it was she herself;

and there is a very wide difference, you know. I hope my little boy was not so rude as to let his amusement at this old woman be seen?"

Ernest hung his head, but he was as truthful as he was thoughtless, and he said in a low voice, "I did laugh, mamma, but it was partly at what Harry Rhoads said."

"And what did he say?" asked Mrs. Kennedy.

"He asked what she'd take for her gunboats," he answered, very low indeed.

Mrs. Kennedy looked sorry. "And is this my little True Knight," she said, "who told me the other day that when he grew up he meant to be another Sir Galahad, and ride through the world protecting all the weak people, and comforting all the sorrowful ones, and punishing all the cruel ones? And he begins by laughing at an old woman, who, from her dress, must be a stranger in a strange land, and joining in a rude and senseless joke about her to her very face!"

The little boy stood silent for a moment, with his face working to keep back the tears, and then he threw himself sobbing into his mother's arms. "Indeed, indeed, I did not think, mamma," he said presently, "but I'll never do it again; and the very next time I see her I'll tell her how sorry I am."

"Now I have my little True Knight again," said his mother, kissing away his tears; "and you will soon have a chance to apologize to the old woman, for I think I know who she is. Mr. Chipman told me the other day that if I wished any washing or cleaning done, he knew of a poor woman who would be very glad to do it; and when I asked him who it was, he said he couldn't possibly pronounce her name, much less spell it, but that he knew where she lived, and that she had lately come from Germany. She has taken that little tumbledown house on the street that Mr. Chipman's store is on, but away out in the fields, and you and I might walk there this afternoon, as we each have an errand to her."

"It must be the same old woman," said Ernest joyfully, "for I saw her go out that very street: and there couldn't be two; do you think there could, mamma?"

"There might possibly be," said his mother, smiling, "but it is not at all probable. Now run and wash your face and hands and smooth your mane, or dinner will be ready for you before you are ready for it."

There was nobody to dispute Ernest's right to the "pull-bone" of the chicken that graced the dinner-table, for he had neither sister nor brother; but by his own request he was helped first to the "drumstick," and just as he was holding out his plate for a second help an idea occurred to him. "Mamma," he said, "do you think— Might I keep the rest of my share of the chicken to take to the old woman? I could finish on bread and gravy, you know; I'm not *near* full yet."

"Yes, I think that would be a very good plan," replied his mother. "I will put it on a plate, and add the vegetables, and some cranberry in a little bowl, and if you wish to make it still better you might give her your dessert."

Ernest hesitated a little. "What is for dessert to-day, mamma?" he asked.

"Peggy's 'queen of puddings,'" answered his mother.

Ernest looked very undecided. Of all Peggy's puddings, the "queen," he thought, best deserved that name. But he suddenly remembered the surprised, distressed face of the poor old woman as she stood among the laughing boys of whom he had been one. "I'll do it, mamma," he said resolutely, "but you'll excuse me, won't you, before the pudding comes in? I'm 'most afraid I couldn't stand it if I were once to see it."

"Very well," said Mrs. Kennedy; "I think that will be a wise thing to do. And don't you think that perhaps 'Lead us not into temptation' means something like this: 'Let us not be led, not stay, where we will be tempted'? You know it is so much easier to give anything up when we go quite away from it, instead of lingering around and looking at it."

"I never thought of that before," said Ernest seriously, "but I'll try to remember it, mamma; and oh, please excuse me, for I hear Peggy coming with the pudding."

It was only to save Peggy's feelings that Mrs. Kennedy ate her share of pudding that day, for she knew how real her boy's self-denial had been, and the "queen" might have been the least of her subjects, for all the pleasure she gave Mrs. Kennedy. But

Peggy was sensitive about the treatment which her dainties received, so a slice was duly eaten, and another, double in size, put into a deep saucer, and then into a basket with the nicely-covered plate containing the dinner, and a pretty napkin spread over the whole.

It was quite a long walk from Mrs. Kennedy's house, which was just outside the town, to the forlorn old hut in which the poor German woman lived; but the day was bright and pleasant, Ernest and his mother had, as usual, a good deal to talk about, and they thought the end of the walk came very soon. They found the old woman at home, busily digging up the little strip of garden in front of her house; and Ernest, who was very much afraid that his courage would fail, whispered to his mother, "Let me speak first, please, mamma."

It was quite evident that the old woman did not recognize him, which made it all the harder, but he "took his courage by both hands," as somebody says, and marched up to her, thinking of Sir Galahad, and

> "My strength is as the strength of ten,
> Because my heart is pure."

He made his best bow, and said resolutely, "I've come to beg your pardon, ma'am. I was very rude, and laughed at you this morning, and I'm truly sorry. Will you please forgive me?" and he held out his hand.

The old woman looked steadily at him for a moment, and then

a great tear rolled down her sunburned face. I will not attempt to write the broken English in which she spoke, but Ernest could understand her quite well, and this is what she said: "And I thought all the little American boys were bad and rude, and here is a little gentleman who asks pardon of an old, poor woman like me!—My dear, I was not angry, only sorry. I said to myself, 'Those little boys do not know what it means to be old and poor and alone, or they would not laugh; they would be more like crying.' But do not feel any trouble; I had forgiven you before, and now, if you will let me, I will love you."

He had been afraid that she would be too angry even to listen to him; he knew how being laughed at had always terribly enraged him; and he looked up at her, saying simply, "I think you must be very good."

"My dear," she answered, "shall I be angry for a little laughing, when my holy Master prayed that His bitter enemies might be forgiven?"

Mrs. Kennedy found old Madelon only too thankful for the promise of work; so when that was settled they had a pleasant talk about gardening and chickens and dogs and cats; and Madelon took them to the shed at the back of her house to show Ernest her two broods of young pigeons, which she intended raising to sell. He was delighted with the pretty little white creatures, and could scarcely talk of anything else all the way home, wondering whether if he should save his weekly six cents until the pigeons were old enough to be taken from the mother-bird, he would have enough money to buy one for his own particular pet.

His knighthood was put to more than one severe test in the weeks which followed. Madelon seemed fated to meet the schoolboys at least two or three times a week, and the howl of derision which greeted Ernest when, a few days after his visit, he took off his cap and spoke to her pleasantly as she passed them, was almost too much for his resolution; but he thought again of Sir Galahad, and of Him for whom Sir Galahad was fighting, and, to his great surprise, the boys soon ceased to ridicule him, and one or two of them even began to say it was "a shame" for the rest "to make fun of the poor old soul." Madelon soon had plenty to do, for Mrs. Kennedy found her so faithful and efficient that she could safely recommend her to others, and the forlorn house began to have a look of neatness and comfort which would have been thought impossible by any one seeing it a few months before.

The time had come when Ernest's mother always took him for the yearly visit to her mother and father, who lived about five miles out of the little city where Ernest's home was. This visit was the greatest delight of the whole year, and was eagerly looked forward to for weeks before the time arrived.

But when this year the day came upon which they were to go, Ernest felt strangely heavy and dull, and his mother began to think something must be the matter when the carriage came for them and he got quietly into it, with none of his usual joyful excitement. There had been several showers during the day, and as they drew near the farm a beautiful rainbow spanned the pond, but Ernest went into no raptures; he merely said, "Yes, it's very pretty, mamma;" and he distressed grandma, after their arrival,

"A BEAUTIFUL RAINBOW SPANNED THE POND."

by eating scarcely any supper and proposing to go to bed immediately afterward, although he had not yet seen the new calf or the kittens. And the next morning, after frightening everybody out of their wits by looking as if he had the small-pox, he relieved their minds by only having chicken-pox.

But he did not think there was any "only" about it, poor little boy! To be shut up in one room with all out-of-doors calling to him to come and enjoy it; to be obliged to postpone indefinitely the visits he had intended making to the calf and the kittens, and the egg-hunting expeditions when the hens were cackling under his window as if they were crazy: it did seem too much. He tried hard to be patient and not to give his mother trouble, but it was difficult work, and he said one day, rather fretfully, "This isn't like being a knight at all, mamma. I don't believe Sir Galahad ever had chicken-pox—do you?"

"I don't know, dear," replied his mother, smiling a little in spite of herself, "but you may be sure he had things to bear that were quite as hard. You know he rode on through the bitter winter nights, never stopping at any of the pleasant homes whose lighted windows he passed; and he was not fighting then, but only enduring, which is much harder. So my little knight must learn to endure too. Don't you remember, when you were looking up all the texts about soldiers and fighting, how much you liked this one: 'Endure hardness as good soldiers of Christ'? Now you have the best possible chance to practise it."

"Mamma, I think you must be Mrs. Interpreter," said Ernest joyfully. "I never thought of it in that way, but I will not grumble another single grumble—you see if I do."

His resolution was sorely tried the very next day. He was growing better rapidly, but not more comfortable, for the bed felt

"GRANDMA SENT BIJOU WITH A BUNCH OF GRAPES." See Page 31.

as if it were stuffed with chestnut-burrs, his eyes were too weak even for looking at pictures, and his restlessness made reading aloud seem tedious.

Grandma sent Bijou, her funny little Skye terrier, with a bunch of white grapes, which he carried carefully by the stem, just as he had been told, and he sat on the bed and offered his paw to Ernest with a very sympathizing face. But the little boy was soon tired even of Bijou. It was a very rainy day, and, tantalizing as it had been to have "those conceited old hens" announcing their eggs under his window, and the birds singing in the cherry tree just outside it, the silence into which the pouring rain had driven them seemed even worse.

A long stretch of open fields lay before his window, with the road from the town winding through it, and it had been one of his amusements to watch the people coming and going, and the farmers bringing their horses to the blacksmith's shop, which stood beside the road. There was a good deal of travel on it during the day, notwithstanding the rain, and Ernest sat up in bed for some time, more interested in two refractory horses, which objected to being shod, than he had been in anything all that dull morning; but after a while his back ached so that he was obliged to lie down again.

"I will count five hundred with my eyes shut, mamma," he said, "before I look any more."

The counting made him drowsy, and he was just dropping into

"TWO REFRACTORY HORSES OBJECTED TO BEING SHOD."

a doze when his mother, who was standing at the window, suddenly exclaimed, "I do believe that is old Madelon coming along the road. Yes, it really is. Why, the poor old soul must have walked all the way from town in this pouring rain; and there is her funny little black dog with her; and—can you see, Ernest?—what it is that she has in her basket? It is something white."

Just then a sudden gust of wind turned Madelon's large umbrella completely inside out; her cap-ribbons—for she seldom wore a bonnet—fluttered wildly in the wind; the white thing in the basket fluttered too; but Madelon and the little black dog, Fritz, plodded steadily on, and reached the gate at last, so dripping wet that no persuasion could make them come farther than the out-kitchen, and even then the old woman apologized humbly for the "muss" that she and Fritz made on the clean brick floor.

Grandmother Russell hastily hunted up some old clothes for Madelon to put on; Fritz made his toilet by a succession of violent shakes; and when both were perfectly dry they were shown into Ernest's room. The basket went too, and in it was the very prettiest white pigeon that he had ever seen. It had a fluffy topknot, a fluffier ruff round its neck, and a fan-tail of which it seemed immensely vain.

It was perfectly tame, and its soft cooing as it fluttered and strutted about the room sounded to Ernest like the sweetest music.

"And you really brought it for me? quite for my own?" he said, putting up his face to give old Madelon the kiss which he considered his warmest expression of thanks.

"For thee, dear little one," answered Madelon with a tender smile; "and I would it were much more, but it is my best."

"But, you poor, dear woman, why did you take this long walk on such a terribly rainy day? and how did you know that Ernest was ill?" asked Mrs. Kennedy, laying her hand kindly on the old woman's shoulder.

"It was Mr. Chipman who told me of the illness," answered

Madelon; "and this was the very first day on which I had not to work; and the rain is not so bad to me, dear madame, as it would be to you, so often I have walked to my work in storms worse than this soft, warm rain, which only wets; it does not freeze and chill. And I said to myself that the little boy would be feeling yet more dull to-day because of the rain, and that even a small thing would amuse him; so Fritz and I walked stoutly on, and here we are. The poor umbrella! it has had the worst."

Grandmother Russell would not hear of Madelon's returning home that night, so she and Fritz were made comfortable with good suppers and good beds; and in the morning, just as she was cheerfully starting on her five-mile walk, long before six o'clock, in order to be in time for her day's work, grandfather drove up to the door in the "Germantown wagon," announcing that he had an early errand to do in town, and that she must allow him the pleasure of taking her home. And when she uncovered the basket in which the white pigeon had travelled, she found one of grandmother's loaves of sweet brown bread and two of her special prints of "grass butter."

And the result of a long "think" which Ernest took just before he went to sleep that rainy evening was this somewhat singular remark: "Mamma, I don't think I'm much of a True Knight; I think it's Madelon."

"IN A MINUTE."

"YOU'LL be sure to call me first, mamma, and then, you know, I can help you get the children ready."

"Yes, dear," said mamma, smiling, for of these "children" one was two years older than Bessy, and the other only a year younger,—"yes, dear, I will call you in time to help me, but I shall be quite satisfied, and a little surprised, if you have yourself ready in time."

"Oh, mamma!" said Bessy reproachfully; "as if I could help being ready for such a day as we're going to have to-morrow!"

"But you know, dear," replied her mother, "how many times,

even pleasant times, you have kept us waiting for one of your 'minutes;' and to-morrow morning, if you are not ready, we must just go without you, for trains and boats are like time and tide—they wait for no man."

"Well, if I don't get right straight up when you call me, mamma," said Bessy, "I wish you would please pinch me, and pull all the bed-clothes off me, and sprinkle cold water in my face."

"I'll help with the pinching and cold-water business," said Rob obligingly; and Ruth added cheerfully, "So will I, Bess."

Mr. and Mrs. Wylie, the father and mother of these three children, had for some years been in the habit of making a little excursion or giving them a picnic on Mrs. Wylie's birthday. Ever since Bessy could remember the day had been marked by a pleasure of this kind, but this year it was to be something quite new and altogether delightful. None of the children had ever seen the ocean, although they lived within ninety miles of it, and this time the excursion was to be taken to Sea-Girt. They were to go by a very early train, and not to leave the beach until seven o'clock in the evening; so there would be the whole delightfully long day by the sea, besides the charming novelty of coming home in an evening train.

You may think it strange that Bessy felt any doubt about being ready for such a day as this, but you would not if you knew what a bad habit she had of putting everything off. Papa called her his "minute-man," because her invariable answer, no matter what she was told or asked to do, was "In a minute." And sometimes the minutes would be multiplied by ten, and sometimes by twenty, or even by thirty or forty.

Mrs. Wylie recommended everybody to go to bed early the night before the excursion. The train was to leave at half-past six, so breakfast must be at six. Then there were the lunch-baskets to be packed, and although everything that could be was ready overnight, some of the preparation must, of course, be left until morning. Ruth and Bessy slept in the same room, their two pretty little bedsteads standing in opposite corners, and there were so much to talk about while they were undressing that when Mrs. Wylie looked in, on her way to her room at nine o'clock, they were still sitting on the floor, gradually taking off their shoes and stockings. But there was time yet for eight hours' good sleep, and they hurried into bed, after repeated requests to their mother to call them not a minute later than five.

They felt as if they had said this about five minutes ago when they were waked by Rob's pounding on the door.

"Mamma says it's five o'clock, girls," he shouted. "She wouldn't let me knock you up before, but I've been dressed for half an hour, and I'm going to the baker's for the rolls right away. Get up, get up, you lazy little things!"

Ruth was out of bed in a minute, and before her eyes were fairly open dressing and chattering all at once. "Oh, Bess," she said, "*do* you think there'll be donkeys? I've been dreaming about it all. I saw them just as plain as plain, and the ocean too, and I'll be so disappointed if there are none, and if it doesn't look like I dreamed it!"

Bessy turned over with her customary morning groan. "Oh

THE DONKEYS OF RUTH'S DREAM.

dear!" she yawned; "I don't hardly think I've been asleep at all. Rob must be mistaken; it can't be five o'clock yet."

"Oh yes it can," answered Ruth briskly, "or Rob wouldn't have said so. Come, Bess: just think how *dreadful* it would be if you were to be too late!"

"It won't take me a whole hour to dress," said Bessy, still more drowsily; "I'll get up in a minute."

"But you know we were to help mamma," said Ruth reproachfully. "Oh, do get up, Bessy! I'll not pinch you, but I'll just tickle you a little;" and Ruth stopped dressing long enough to give Bessy a vigorous tickle. But Bessy only smiled lazily, and did not even open her eyes.

By the time Ruth was nearly dressed Rob was pounding on the door again.

"It's half-after," he called, "and I've got the rolls—three dozen of 'em, magnificent big fellows. Come; you're dreadfully slow this morning."

"Oh, Rob," said Ruth anxiously. "I can't make Bess get up. What shall I do?"

"You let me in there for a minute and *I'll* start her."

"Very well," answered Ruth, opening the door; "but what will you do?"

"Sprinkle her," said Rob; whereat, with a dismal howl, Bessy buried her head under the bed-clothes, and no persuasions from Ruth or Rob could bring it out again, but a smothered voice said angrily, "It's too soon to get up; just let me alone. I won't get up while you plague me so."

At that moment Mrs. Wylie was heard calling from the foot of the stairs, "Come, children, breakfast's ready; come at once, or you'll be late."

Ruth and Rob gave Bessy a parting shake and hurried down stairs.

"Why, where's Bessy?" asked Mrs. Wylie as they sat down to breakfast.

"We've done everything we could, mamma," said Rob: "we've shaken and talked to her, but she won't budge."

Mrs. Wylie looked worried. "I would have come to call her myself," she said, "but I thought I heard you all talking and laughing together, and made my mind quite easy; and if I stop to wake her and help her get ready now, we shall all be left, for there is no time to spare."

Fifteen minutes later Bessy was waked from a delicious nap by the closing of the front door. Scarcely knowing what she did, she sprang out of bed with a little cry, and, still half asleep, put on her white frock, tied her sash, as she always did, in front, and then "worked" it round into place. This fully waked her, and she realized that the people walking quickly toward the station, armed with baskets and umbrellas, were her mother and father and Ruth and Rob. And when the kind-hearted Irish girl who was Mrs. Wylie's only servant came up

"BESSY SAT FORLORNLY ON THE BED."

"SHE SEATED ONE OF THE DOLLS ON HER LAP" See Page 63.

a few minutes later to see about the little girl, as Mrs. Wylie had charged her to do, she found Bessy sitting forlornly on the bed, her night-cap still on her curly head, and her bare feet sticking out from her clean white dress.

"Come, dear, and get your breakfast," said Katty soothingly. "They left you the full of a basket of all the fine things they had, and your mamma said I might picnic you out under the big tree."

At first Bessy felt as if she should never eat anything more in her whole life, but when she had taken her bath, and Katty had helped her to dress, and she found the little table temptingly spread under the walnut tree, she changed her mind and made a very good breakfast, with her doll and Ruth's perched up in two chairs for company. But they were very silent company, and during the long day that followed she did some of the best thinking she had ever done in her little life. For the day seemed as if it would never come to an end. She lingered as long as she could over her breakfast. Then she took a new story-book, which Ruth and she had been reading together, and, seating one of the dolls on her lap, offered amiably to read aloud to her. But the doll's stupid stare and blank silence were too painfully in contrast with Ruth's animated face and merry comments on the story, so she soon gave it up, and wandered out of doors again. And now she saw clearly, for the first time, how much unhappiness she was giving as well as taking. She had never before acknowledged, even to herself, that most of the "unpleasantness" about the house was owing to her: she always thought, if she did not say, that some one else was to blame, and she had spoken of her bad habit as if it were a lame leg or a broken arm—something for which she was to be pitied rather than blamed. And she certainly was to be pitied, but not exactly in the manner which she required. She had more than many children have to make her happy and comfortable, but she succeeded in making herself—and, what was worse, a number of other people—anything but comfortable the greater part of the time; for somebody who is never ready, and never does her share of the lifting and pulling until she is absolutely obliged to, even if she is a very small somebody, can spoil a good many things. She made a very earnest and prayerful resolve to fight this dragon of slothfulness; and by way of a good beginning she offered to set the table for the late supper, so that, when the picnic-party came home, sunburnt and tired and hungry, it did not find Bessy fretful and injured, but very gentle and penitent and humble.

She is having a hard fight with her dragon, but it helps her greatly to think that the great apostle who charges us to be "fervent in spirit, serving the Lord," thought it worth while also to charge us to be "not slothful in business."

THE TRAVELS OF A CHRISTMAS TREE.

IT was Christmas Eve, and from sweet-toned bells in many parts of the great city came joyful notes, now chiming out a tune, now ringing peals and catches, until the frosty-looking stars seemed twinkling back the sounds to the glistening, newly-fallen snow. Windows full of wonderful things, which Santa Claus had not yet had time to collect, glittered and shone in the gaslight, the tinkle of sleigh-bells was everywhere, and there was such a joyous stir and bustle among the people crowding the streets that it was hard to realize that underneath it all there were want and sadness in many hearts and homes.

The windows drew about them eager faces which were so small that one knew they must be children's faces, but which were old in sorrow or sin, or both. But among them were some still fresh and cheerful and pleasant. Before the brilliant show in the window of a great toyshop stood a tall, slender young girl, whose honest face wore a steady, settled look, as if she had had more responsibility than usually falls to one so young. On her arm she held a rosy-cheeked baby boy some two or three years old, and a little girl of five or six was holding her skirt.

They had been " choosing," without the least regard to the probable cost, until nearly everything in the window was chosen; then, with a little laugh that ended in a sigh, the older sister turned away, saying, "Come, Polly; if we choose so much, Santa Claus won't bring anything. Dick is half asleep now, and you know I have the meat to buy yet, and the medicine for mother."

"Oh, but, Rena," said the little girl, "I haven't finished. I choose that picture for mother, and that great big jumping-jack for Dick, and that workbox for you, and—"

"Come, leave the poor shopman a little," said Rena gayly. "I am very much obliged for my workbox, and I will mend all your clothes out of it; but Dick is sleepy, and is growing heavier every minute, and mother is all alone, you know, and she will want her tea."

"Do you think we are going to have money enough for just a little, little tree?" asked Polly earnestly. "See, there's the poor old man who has been trying to sell them all day. His nose looks quite frozen, and he has tied his handkerchief over his ears. Let's ask him how much it is for the very smallest one."

"We must wait till the other things are bought, dear," answered Rena. "Here we are at the butcher's, and the drug-store is just across the way; we will soon know."

When the joint of meat for the Christmas dinner and the bottle

"RENA ONCE MORE COUNTED THE MONEY IN HER HAND"   See page 69

of medicine for the sick mother were paid for, there were just ten cents left.

"I'm afraid we can't get even a little tree for that," said Rena as they came to the corner where the old man still stood rubbing his benumbed hands together in a vain effort to warm them, "but I'll ask him.—Have you any smaller trees in the wagon, sir?"

"Now, what would anybody want with a smaller tree than that?" said the old man, rather crossly. He was very cold, and he had not sold as many trees as he had hoped to, and he was wishing himself beside the fire at home.

"It was only because of the price," replied Rena, humbly. "I haven't much money left, and I was afraid this little tree, with the cross-piece to make it stand, might cost more than I had, so I thought perhaps you had some in the wagon without it."

"And so I have, my dear," said the old man in a much pleasanter tone, "but I'm afraid I shall not sell even these to-night, and I'd sooner give you the one with the stand for the price of one without it than unload any more. You can have that smallest one for fifteen cents; and sure that's cheap enough."

Rena with a very grave face once more counted the money in her hand, but no counting could make it more than ten cents.

"Yes, I suppose it is cheap," she answered sadly, "but I've only ten cents left."

"You might run home and bring the other five," suggested the old man; "I'll wait for you here."

"Thank you, that is very kind," replied Rena, "but this is all we can spare. I'm sorry, for we've always had a tree before. Good-night, sir, and a happy Christmas to you!" and Rena stooped to lift the basket from the shelter of the little trees.

"Wait a minute, my dear, and don't be so hasty," said the old man. "There's a saying that 'A bird in the hand is worth two in the bush.' Very likely I'll sell no more trees to-night, and then all to-morrow I'll be thinking that I might have made ten cents more; so take it along: it's so small that the little one there can easily carry it."

"Oh, thank you very much," said Rena joyfully.—"Here, Polly, hold it in your arms, so.—I *hope* you'll have a happy Christmas sir; good-night."

"Happy Christmas, sir—good-night," echoed Polly.

"The same to you, my dears, and here's an end of the tied greens to go over your looking-glass;" and the old man hung a pretty green coil round Polly's neck.

With fresh thanks and good wishes Rena and Polly started briskly for home; and the invalid mother's face brightened at sight of the cheerful green things and on hearing about the old man's kindness.

"He put something in my coat-pocket when he hung the wreath round my neck," said Polly, pulling off her mittens to search out the mystery.—"Why, Rena, it's the ten cents! Oh, the dear, kind old gentleman! Now we can have five little candles for the tree.

Please go quickly, Rena, and buy them, and we'll have it all lighted when father comes home."

Rena went very willingly, having first unwrapped the sleepy baby and laid him beside his mother on the bed; and by the time the tired father, discouraged with one more fruitless search for work, came slowly up the stairs, the little tree's five candles were burning cheerily. Rena and Polly told him all about it as they flew around setting the table and dishing the hot mush for supper, and he quite agreed with them about the kindness of the gift. He hung the wreath over the door before they sat down to supper, and the candles were carefully blown out, that they might last for another lighting. Rena, with a significant look at her father and Polly, poured a few spoonfuls of milk over the plate of mush which she carried to her mother; the rest of them ate it with no sauce but that of a good, hearty appetite.

"That isn't bad after the tramp I've had to-day," said the father, helping himself to another plateful.

" And no work yet, father?" asked Rena.

" No, my dear," he answered sadly. " They read Mr. Hutton's letter in several places, and were very civil and very sorry, but had nothing for me to do. But we'll try not to fret Christmas away. It's been running in my mind all day, 'Trust in the Lord, and be doing good; dwell in the land, and verily thou shalt be fed.' It goes against me to use your little savings, daughter, but with those and your wages we can pull through for two or three weeks more;

and surely by that time a man who is willing to do anything honest can find something to do."

"Of course he can," said the mother's weak voice, cheerfully; "and you haven't counted me. You'll see when you eat your dinner to-morrow, and when the little tree blazes up again, that I didn't learn to crochet for nothing."

"Bless your dear heart! there's no putting *you* down;" and her husband left the table to give her a hearty kiss.

"Is there any mush left, Rena?" asked the mother.

"Yes, mother," answered Rena, scraping it into a bowl; "I can take a little of the beef-fat and fry it for breakfast."

"I know something better than that to do with it," said the father. "I don't believe that poor little soul on the floor above has tasted anything hot to-day; it's all her mother can do to get bread for them and keep a little fire.—Run up with what's left, Polly, and tell her to eat it while it's hot; folks who are going to have such a dinner as your mother's hinting at can afford to eat bread for breakfast."

Polly skipped up stairs with the bowl of mush, and was gone ten or fifteen minutes. When she came back with the empty bowl she was half crying. "It's all dark but what comes in from the street," she said, "and Jeanie is all by herself. Her mother had to go away off with some work, and she says they've only bread for dinner to-morrow, and that if they buy any candles they won't have that; and I don't see why they can't light the gas."

"I suppose because they can't pay for it, dear," said the mother. "Did Jeanie like the mush?"

"She said it was too good for anything," answered Polly gleefully, her little face changing suddenly from tears to smiles, "and she kept half of it for her mother. Oh, suppose we give her the tree?"

"You shall if you like, darling, and if Rena is willing," said the mother. "Dick is too little to be consulted, even if he were awake."

"Of course I'm willing," said Rena brightly. "The little tree has shone for us, and now it can go and shine for Jeanie.—We'll light it again, Polly, and carry it up so."

When Jeanie's tired mother came home with the little sum for which she had walked so far, and which must be spread out over a whole week, she heard singing; two thin little voices were piping out—

> "Carol, carol, Christians,
> Carol joyfully;
> Carol for the coming
> Of Christ's nativity.
> Carol! ca-rol!"

And when she opened the door, instead of finding a dark room and a lonely little daughter, she found two carollers, and the little tree shining in the corner of the room, with one white, one red, one yellow, one blue, and one green candle interspersed among its spreading branches.

Polly said good-night and ran down stairs, and Jeanie's mother drew from under her shawl a whole pound of candles.

"Oh, where did you get them? I'm so glad!" cried Jeanie joyfully; "I hate to sit in the dark."

"Mr. Chipman gave them to me when I paid his bill," answered Jeanie's mother. "He's the best man alive, I do believe, and I suppose he's noticed that I haven't bought any lately. Now we can light one and save your tree for another night. I don't know yet where you got it."

So Jeanie told about the mush and Polly and the tree, and the poor widow's heart grew warm as she listened: times were hard, and keeping alive was a struggle, but the feeling of loneliness which had oppressed her all day was gone.

"If I were a rich woman," she said as she lighted the one candle and put out the five, "the person I'd see to first would be that little lame child across the entry. I caught sight of her face as I came in, and I can't get it out of my head; she'll not live long if they can't feed her a little better."

"Do you believe they've any Christmas over there?" asked Jeanie with a quick glance at the tree.

"No, indeed, poor souls!" said her mother. "They'll be thankful for one meal to-morrow, let alone three, and I don't believe they've had more than one to-day."

"Then I know what I'm going to do." Jeanie spoke quickly, as if she did not wish to think. "I'm going to light my tree again

"HAPPY LITTLE CHILDREN WOKE TO SEARCH THEIR STOCKINGS."

See Page 71

and give it to her. Polly won't care—she's too good—and I can always see it if I shut my eyes." And, springing up, she relit the five little candles, now burnt half away, and slowly and carefully carried the tree across the entry.

The pale little cripple started up with a rapturous " Oh !" at sight of the tree, and when Jeanie explained that she was to keep it, and that it would be pretty and green for days after the candles were burnt away, the wan face was lifted for a kiss, and then the child lay with folded hands, gazing at the tree. "It smells like the woods we went to once," she murmured.—" Oh, mammy, look! don't you care ?"

The sullen, hard-looking woman raised her head, and her face softened, "Yes, my dear, it's rarely pretty," she said, more kindly than she had spoken for days ; and Jeanie, well satisfied, stole out of the room.

"Will you put it out now, mother, so that it may burn a little to-morrow night ?" asked the child.

As her mother rose to do it a woman who lived in one of the lower rooms came in without the ceremony of knocking. " Poor old granny's going fast," she said, " and I came to see if you'd that prayer-book that used to be on the table. She's begging of us to pray with her, and she seems so distressed I thought I'd try to read her a prayer, even if they made game of me for it. She's wandering like, and keeps saying bits of hymns about Christmas, and talking to her children, poor soul! and they all dead and gone years ago! She's said a dozen times, 'Light the tree, father, and then call them in.'"

The little cripple rose on her bed. "Oh, Mrs. Keely," she said eagerly, "carry her down my tree. She'll think it's her children's. Do, please."

"You poor little soul!" said the kind-hearted woman; "it's the only sign of Christmas you've got or are likely to get; you'd better keep it."

"Indeed, I'd rather she'd have it, please," she said, so earnestly that Mrs. Keely yielded, and the wistful eyes followed the tree out of the door and along the entry until the stairs swallowed it up. The mother had silently handed Mrs. Keely the prayer-book.

The dying eyes grew strangely bright as the little tree twinkled before them, and the feeble voice murmured,

> "'In the silent midnight
> Centuries ago.'"

That was all.

"She's with the children now, poor dear!" said Mrs. Keely softly, "and I'll take the tree back to the poor little girl; it'll comfort her, maybe, and it can't do granny any more good."

Christmas Day dawned brightly, and the happy little children in warm, comfortable homes woke to search their well-filled stockings and to rejoice over the many gifts prepared by loving hearts and hands. But to those of whom I have been telling you no more of the outward part of Christmas came than the small share which had come on Christmas Eve. Yet they were not unhappy; the Christmas love and warmth were in their hearts; and

> "The heart aye's the part aye
> That sets us right or wrong."

Perhaps the happiest of them all was the little cripple, whose tree, standing in the one window of the room, wafted its wild-wood

"ONE OF THE LADIES OF THE FLOWER MISSION BROUGHT HER A BUNCH OF ROSES."

fragrance to the child, until, shutting her eyes, she "made believe" she was in the woods once more. Day after day the sun made shadows of her tree for her on the floor of her room—beautiful out-of-doors shadows. The worn, hard face of the despairing mother grew softer, her voice gentler, as she sat at her ceaseless work in the shadow of the Christmas tree.

Not until one of the kind ladies of the Flower Mission brought the little cripple a bunch of glowing roses did she give up the dingy and yellow pine-bough which had been such a delight to her; and then, not willing that it should be thrown into the muddy street, she begged her mother to burn it.

Dear little hearts, when Christmas comes again is there nothing you can do to send into cheerless homes a share of the Christmas joy?

HOME WITH THE TIDE.

ALL night the storm had beaten
    Like thunder on the rock,
And the mother's heart had trembled
    And sunk with every shock;
And closer she held her baby,
    Whispering, "Ah, by dawn
Thou may'st be an orphan, little one—
    Thy father may be gone."

The storm died into silence
    As daylight slowly broke,
And with laughter and with crooning
    The little baby woke.
The mother, worn with watching,
    Gathered him on her arm:
"We will go to the beach, my baby, and see
    If the storm has wrought us harm."

She sat on a rock and waited,
    But she looked not toward the sea;
She only asked the fishers,
    "Have you any news for me?"

And she watched old Ailie gathering
　　Moss from the rocks below.
" Her man was drowned," the young wife thought,
　" And her two lads, long ago."

"SHE SAT ON A ROCK AND WAITED."

But a merry shout from the fishers
　　Raised the sad eyes suddenly;
A little boat rode gayly
　　Over the tossing sea.

Fast as the wind could bring her
  She came with her sail spread wide.
"Oh, baby! father is coming!"
  The happy mother cried;
And she held her baby up to look—
  "He's coming home with the tide."

COURAGE.

PERHAPS there are about six boys in all Christendom who are really glad when holidays are over and school begins again, but the boys who belonged to Mr. Brainard's school were a good deal less sorry than most schoolboys are. There were only about twelve of them, and Mrs. Brainard knew each one, and mothered all; and it must be a very lazy and unambitious boy who was not roused to interest in his studies by Mr. Brainard.

The summer vacation of the school was over, most of the boys had returned, and Jack Lyman, who was among the older ones, had just driven up to the door in Mr. Brainard's light wagon with a small boy and a large trunk. Jack liked driving, and was often trusted with the steady old horse which Mr. Brainard kept chiefly for journeys to and from the station. Mrs. Brainard came out to welcome the new-comer, while some of the smaller boys gathered round. The little fellow was so slender, and his face was so small and thin, that Mrs. Brainard's motherly heart was touched with pity for him.

"I am glad to see you, dear," she said, taking his hand with a warm clasp in both her own.—" Boys, this is Everard Phillips; he is the only 'new boy' this term, and you must all do the honors

"MRS. BRAINARD CAME OUT TO WELCOME THE NEW-COMER."

of the school. Remember how strange it seemed to you at first, and try to make the new member of our family feel at home."

"It didn't seem strange to *me* long after I saw you, Mrs. Brainard," said Jack Lyman with his pleasant smile, "and I don't believe it will to him; it sha'n't if we can help it;" and he put his hand kindly on the little fellow's shoulder."

Mrs. Brainard smiled brightly in return. "Thank you, Jack," she said; and then, turning toward the two smallest boys, one of whom was hiding behind her and peeping at the new-comer, she introduced them to him, saying with a loving smile, "These are my own two little sons, Alan and Rob; and now we will go in and you shall be introduced to their small sister, of whom we are all very proud, for she is the only girl among a baker's dozen of boys."

"He looks like a girl in boy's clothes," said Ned Lane contemptuously as soon as Mrs. Brainard and the new boy were out of hearing. "I wonder if he does his hair himself or if he's to have a maid?"

"Oh, come, now, Lane," said Jack good-naturedly; "we can't all be as powerful as you are, and I hope you won't chaff him: his mother died a month or two ago, and he's just been very ill, but he'll soon pick up here; and I dare say Mrs. Brainard will have his hair cut."

"I'll not hurt him," said Ned with a grin which did not quite agree with his words, "but a little bracing up will be good for him."

Master Ned's ideas of "bracing up" were peculiar, and the new boy was soon the object of as many small annoyances as Ned felt it safe to offer him. On learning his name, Ned persisted in calling him "Evie" and "Miss Phillips," and made so many sarcastic allusions to his hair that the little fellow soon asked and obtained permission to have it cut close. Jack stood between Everard and

"A SUDDEN GUST OF WIND TOOK OFF EVERARD'S CAP."

his tormentor whenever he could, and was pleased with the quiet manliness which the little fellow showed; he rarely answered Ned's taunts, and, but for the quick flush which passed over his face, seemed not to mind them.

School was just out one windy day in March, and the day-scholars, of whom there were five or six, were starting for their homes. Several of the boarders went a little way with them, and among these were Jack, Ned, and Everard. The latter had grown both taller and stouter, and would scarcely have been recognized as the pale and thin little little fellow who had come in the fall; but he was still very quiet and reserved, except to Mrs. Brainard and Jack, and cared more for books than for play. A sudden gust of wind took off his cap, and he tried in vain to catch it; successive puffs sent it flying along the road, and finally into a pool of muddy water. One of the day-scholars good-naturedly helped him to fish it out, but it was soaked and spoiled. Everard's "Thank you" was said with trembling lips, and the boys, to their utter astonishment, saw that his eyes were full of tears.

Ned gave a loud whoop, and then said, with mock sympathy, "And did its little cap get wet? Never mind, we'll hang it up to dry."

And, seizing the cap before Everard could prevent him, he was about to toss it into a tree when Jack grasped him by the shoulder, saying sternly, "You drop that! Give it back to him if you know what's good for you."

"You needn't grab me like that; it's none of *your* business, anyhow," said Ned sullenly, but at the same time "shying" the cap at

Everard with such good aim that it struck him full in the face. The little fellow turned without a word and ran home.

Jack's grasp tightened and his lips were white with his effort at self-control as he said, "If I catch you bullying that boy just once more, Ned Lane, I'll give you the thrashing you ought to have had some time ago; as it is, I'm so strongly tempted to duck you that I'd advise you to take the temptation out of my sight;" and he flung Ned from him rather forcibly. Ned hesitated a moment, and then walked away crestfallen. Jack's easy good-nature had misled him, at the beginning of their acquaintance, into presuming upon it, and he had still a wholesome recollection of the consequences.

Jack went in search of Everard, whom he at last found in one of the dormitories with his face hidden in his pillow.

"Oh, come, now," said Jack cheerfully; "I wouldn't take that pup's behavior so hard if I were you. I think I've settled him for a while anyhow, and, if you'll let me say so, you ought to try not to give way so before him; it gives him a sort of clinch on you, don't you see? And nobody will haul you up about the cap; Mrs. Brainard never makes a fuss about things of that kind."

"It's not that," said Everard with a quivering voice. "You're very kind, Jack, but you don't understand. Mother made me that cap only a month before—" He did not finish the sentence, but after a few minutes' pause he said: "It was the very last thing she made me. We were away in the country, and I had spoiled all my hats and caps somehow, and she took a piece of cloth she had brought to embroider on, and made this one all herself, without even a pattern; and she was so proud of it! I've been meaning to put it away, for fear something would happen to it, but it seemed to me that while I wore it I was nearer somehow— I can't explain it."

"I understand," said Jack softly. "I beg your pardon with all my heart. And I just want to tell you something: you're coming to spend your summer vacation with me if you've no plan you like better for it. Mrs. Brainard's a lovely woman, but the mother had a little baby that died ever so long ago, before I was born, and she's been mothering everybody she could get hold of ever since, I do believe."

Everard's cheerfulness increased rapidly after this talk, and he was never weary of hearing Jack tell about his home and "the mother."

The precious cap was carefully cleaned and dried, and then, by Jack's advice, locked safely away in Everard's bureau; and Ned, who was much more thoughtless than malicious, and who did not wish to have a quarrel with a boy so popular as Jack was, took care to let Everard alone when the latter was present, knowing well that Everard would not report to him the remarks made in his absence.

Mrs. Brainard's baby May was the pet and plaything of all the boys, boarders and day-scholars; there were lively contentions for the honor of pushing her coach and giving her pickaback and shoulder rides; and she returned the general affection with a perfect trustfulness in everybody's goodwill which had more influence over the boys than they themselves knew. She patted their heads, whenever she could reach them, exactly as she caressed the large black dog which was nearly always with her, and, as she had no favorites, she had no enemies; her faith in dogs and boys had never been shaken. Mrs. Brainard generally stayed within call when the small queen was among her rough subjects, but one afternoon it happened that Mr. Brainard needed her help with some of his school-work; the nurse was away, and she stood undecided what to do. The day was so bright and warm that she disliked to bring the baby in-doors, and she knew, besides, that her ladyship would accept no divided service, and that an attempt at helping Mr. Brainard with Baby May in the room would only succeed in hindering him. The boys had been playing rather actively, and were now resting in the shade, and as soon as they understood her perplexity she had plenty of volunteers.

"She'll be pulled to pieces if I give her to all of you to take care of," said Mrs. Brainard, with the loving smile which had helped to win her so many hearts; "so I must make a special appointment of three, as I did the last time I was in distress. I will take the three nearest to the throne: Ned, Charlie, Everard, you can relieve guard for each other; it will only be for an hour, and if you want me you will find me in the library. I don't know where Lion is, or he would help you."

Lion, who was the large dog aforesaid, knew very well where he was: somebody had thoughtlessly shut him into one of the recitation-rooms, which was on the second floor, and his mind was divided between risking a jump from the open window and raising a howl that should also raise the house.

"Keep her quite away from the pond, please," Mrs. Brainard turned to say as she was entering the house: "she has had a desire within the last few days to go 'fissing,' she tells me, and she is so daring that I am in constant terror about her."

The boys were soon tired of doing nothing, and when one of them suggested that it was cooler in the barn, and that a game of "Follow my Leader" could be played there as well as out of doors, the rest started up with alacrity, with the exception of the little queen's body-guard. Ned and Charlie grumbled a little, but Everard, who was deep in a book of fairy-stories, scarcely heard them until Charlie exclaimed, "I say, Everard, you've been reading ever since Mrs. Brainard went in, and haven't taken your share: suppose you take it now, and Ned and I will be back in half an hour and let you off to your book again."

"Very well," said Everard, to whom the arrangement seemed quite fair; and he rather reluctantly closed the book.

Baby May had been sitting contentedly in her chariot, playing with a string of bright beads and chattering to the audience in general, and she was not at all pleased when the audience unceremoniously left her to her own devices. She immediately asked to

"LION WAS ALREADY PULLING BABY MAY FROM THE WATER."

See Page 95.

be taken "fissing;" and Everard, to keep her from fretting, fastened a bit of paper to a string, and the string to a stick, and told her to fish over the side of her carriage. This was something entirely new and delightful, and she entered into it with spirit, laughing gleefully every time she landed her fish.

"I'll just finish this story: there's only a little left, and I *must* see how he got out of the cavern," said Everard to himself as he opened his book once more, answering the scruple which rose in his conscience at the idea of neglecting his trust in this way. The baby's perfect contentment beguiled him into beginning another story, and he was soon so entirely absorbed that he had forgotten everything else; and little May might have made much more noise than she did without rousing him when she softly let herself down over the side of her carriage—an accomplishment which she had very lately acquired—and stole away to the pond on the other side of the house.

The child's shrill scream and an answering roar from Lion roused him suddenly from his book, but before he could think almost the great dog had leaped from the window, gathered himself up from the grass, and rushed toward the pond; and when Everard reached the bank Lion was already pulling Baby May from the water. Charlie and Ned, true to their promise, had been returning to "relieve guard" as the dog leaped from the window, and all three boys stood in silent dismay as Lion gently drew the dripping baby up the bank.

Then Ned broke out angrily, as he gathered up the sobbing child and started for the house: "You've made a fine mess of it! Mrs. Brainard will blame all three of us alike, and say we're not fit to be trusted, when I suppose the fact is you went on reading as soon as our backs were turned, and didn't care what became of the baby."

Everard made no answer; he only hastened on to meet Mrs. Brainard, who came toward them pale and frightened, for she had heard May's scream.

"Don't stop me with explanations," she said as he tried to speak; "give me my baby."

A warm bath and a good rubbing saved the little lady from any ill effects of her adventure, and when she was asleep, and it was evident that she had taken no harm, Mrs. Brainard sent for the three boys.

Everard had felt no hesitation when he had tried to explain the accident to her at first, but the hour's delay had changed his feeling. He was tempted to allow the other boys to share the blame —to say that they should not have left the baby any more than he should have read—and, above all, not to screen his enemy. But when it came to this the tide turned: his mother's gentle teaching came back to him, and he resolutely put down the temptation, and, with a silent prayer for strength, spoke before any question could be asked.

"Ned and Charlie are not to blame, Mrs. Brainard," he said; "it was all my fault. I was taking my turn—they had taken theirs—and I got to reading when I knew I shouldn't, and I never heard her slip away, nor anything, till I heard her scream; and if she'd been drowned—" He stopped, unable to go on.

"And I felt so sure I could trust you!" said Mrs. Brainard sorrowfully. "That is the worst of all. Baby is not hurt, but if— Oh, Everard, I am afraid it will be a long time before I can trust you again."

"I suppose it will," said Everard humbly, "but if you can only say you forgive me, Mrs. Brainard, I can go to work to make you willing to trust me again."

Nobody who asked in earnest ever asked twice for forgiveness here, and Mrs. Brainard's warm "I do forgive you, dear," and her loving kiss, gave Everard fresh hope and courage.

When the three boys were outside the door, Ned threw his arm across Everard's shoulder. "You've faced the music like a man," he said; "I don't believe *I* could have done it. I'd have thought a third of the blame quite as much as I could shoulder. I'm not much of a speech-maker, but I will say this: I'll go to Jack and ask him to thrash me, and then throw me into the pond, the next time I catch myself bullying you."

THE first of June was little Milly Graham's birthday, and she thought it the loveliest day of the whole year. This was partly because, in many ways, it really was—partly because, ever since she could remember, so many things had been done to make her happy on that day that she must have been a very cross-grained little girl indeed if she had not been as happy as she was meant to be. She was a little only daughter, and for fear she should feel lonesome, with neither brother nor sisters for playmates, her father and mother had given her as many pets as one small girl could well attend to. First in her affections among these came her two dogs, the big St. Bernard, Prince, and the little King Charles, Frisk, and these two seldom left her. Prince evidently felt responsible for her, and did not like to have her out of his sight, and Frisk needed so much petting that he felt used hardly when he was kept out of the schoolroom every morning until Milly's lessons were done. Then, besides the dogs, there were always two or three cats, and there was a rabbit-hutch full of rabbits, and another hutch full of guinea-pigs; so, you see, Milly had her hands full, for it was her delight to feed and care for all these creatures herself. She allowed

MILLY, PRINCE, AND FRISK.

the gardener to help her if she needed help, as she sometimes did— when, for instance, the rabbits would insist upon burrowing out of the hutch, and a fresh trench had to be dug around the walls of their castle and filled with coal-ashes; and she always consulted him and followed his advice if any of her family were ill, so that there was a great friendship between them, and the gardener, whose name was Peter, could always be trusted to feed and care for the animals if Milly were away. For caged birds she had never cared—it troubled her to see winged creatures shut in such narrow prisons and deprived of all their rights and privileges—but she had a large family of table-boarders in the way of birds who came every morning to a great flat stone on the southern side of the house, knowing well that, no matter what the weather might be, they would find their table brushed clean and well supplied with grain and crumbs, and once a week a salad, for Milly had quite a large bed of chickweed under the flower-stands in the green-house, which was allowed to grow expressly for her pensioners, although Peter sometimes protested that it would be only fair to put up a sign explaining why it was there, as it was a great discredit to his gardening.

Milly's first recollection of a birthday—and it was a very misty one—was connected with a box of gilt-and-white china, large enough for a tea-party of the most grown-up dolls, which her mother had spread on a small round table before Milly's wondering eyes, and of a great tumbler of ice-cream which her father had set in the midst of the saucers, giving her a spoon to "help" it with. And there were saucers enough for her to share her birthday-treat with her mother and father, her nurse and the cook and the housemaid and Peter.

That was when she was four years old: now she was eight, and this birthday was to be celebrated in a new and delightful way. Milly's home was in a large town which was almost a city, but the house had plenty of ground around it, and although her mother and father sometimes took her in the summer to the seashore or the mountains, the house was never closed. But better than any new place did Milly love the old farm where her mother had once lived, and where two aunts and two uncles lived still. The lovely old-fashioned house stood within sound of the sea, and here Milly and her mother and father were going, as they did every summer, for a visit of several weeks. But this year the uncles and aunts had begged that the visit might begin with the birthday, and hinted at so many delightful ways of spending birthdays that Milly was on tiptoe with expectation, and stood at the gate for at least ten minutes waiting for the large carriage which was to take them all to the farm. It came at last, and on so lovely a day the drive did not seem long, even to an impatient little person. Prince and Frisk had been included in the invitation, and Prince bounded along, now in front and now behind, while Frisk gave impatient little barks at being obliged to sit still in the carriage.

The climbing rose which half covered the front of the farm-house was in fullest bloom, and Milly thought the old home had never looked so lovely as when the carriage drew up to the gate and she sprang eagerly out. A very warm welcome awaited them, and then Milly could scarcely wait to be put into her clean gingham frock and white apron before she was let loose to explore the

"THE CARRIAGE DREW UP TO THE GATE, AND SHE SPRANG EAGERLY OUT."

place and see whether any changes had occurred since the year before.

"Don't be gone too long," said Aunt Mary, smiling; "somebody is coming to spend the day. Just run and look at the new swing in the barn, and your seat among the hazel-bushes, and your 'Swiss Family Robinson' apple tree, and by that time I think Hatty will be here. Nelly will come to tea, but she is going to school, you know, and couldn't come for the day."

Hatty and Nelly were two pleasant little neighbors with whom Milly had played a great deal the summer before, and she clapped her hands with delight when she heard they were coming, exclaiming, "Oh, Aunt Mary, how *very* kind that was!"

The "Swiss Family Robinson apple tree" was a tree with low-hanging, widespread boughs, in which Uncle George had built her a wonderful summer-house, large enough to hold five or six people: he had put a little table and six little chairs in it; it had charming latticed windows which opened like shutters, and was reached by a sort of combined step-and-rope ladder which could be drawn up in case of siege. On many a wet day he had bundled Milly up in an old shawl and taken her for a visit to the apple-tree house, where certain dolls lived all the year round, and others for the summer only. Now, as her head rose above the ladder-stair, she saw a beautiful little basket on the table. It was twined with flowers, and a card was tied with blue ribbon to the handle; and as Milly bent over it she saw it was full of large white eggs, and on the card was written in large round hand, "Milly," and underneath her name,

"Old Mrs. Speckle humbly begs
You will accept her freshest eggs."

Milly clapped her hands delightedly. "Why, that's the poor old hen I fished out of the water-butt!" she said aloud. Taking the pretty basket on her arm, she went carefully down the stairs and hurried to the barn. There hung the new swing, made of stout rope and with a sort of low chair for a seat. A bundle was tied to one arm of the chair, with another blue-ribboned card upon it, inscribed "Milly," and this time Milly read,

> "Your warm friend Rover begs that you'll adorn
> This hammock, where you'll never find a thorn."

The hammock was long and strong and fine, made of prettily-colored sea-grass; hooks were fitted into the ends, and Milly did not have to look far to find the rings and staples arranged for swinging it.

"He's given it to me because I pulled the thorn out of his foot," she said. "It's just like a fairy-story, and I'm going to pretend all day that it's *perfectly* true. I wonder what I'll find in the hazel-bush seat?" and she hurried off to see.

The seat had been freshly painted and the bushes trimmed into a sort of arbor around it. Two mysterious-looking bundles lay on the seat—a round high one, and a long narrow one. The round one was opened first, and was found to contain two pasteboard boxes. The top box held one of the dainty little cream cheeses which Milly never saw anywhere except at Sweetbrier Farm; and once more there was a verse:

> "Dear little Milly, you'll surely not
> Refuse this cheese from your grateful Spot?

"ROVER AND DOUGLAS AND THE CAT AND THE KITTEN WATCHED HER."

See Page 108.

> You'll eat it soon, if you'll let me advise,
> Before it is carried off by the flies."

"Why, Spot's the cow that I used to keep the flies off of at milking-time because she had a sore ear!" exclaimed Milly; "and oh, what's this?" as she opened the second box. It was a beautiful frosted cake, with her name and the date in pink sugar, and eight candles, of different colors, arranged on the top, all ready for lighting. This time there was no verse on the card; it only said: "For our dear little Milly, with two heartsful of love, from Aunt Mary and Aunt Kitty."

Milly was almost too much overcome to open the long parcel, but not quite; and there lay a lovely wax-headed lady with long fair curls and tranquilly-closed eyes. Milly raised her gently, as if fearing to wake her, and the soft blue eyes flew open with so life-like an expression that Milly hugged her rapturously to her heart. Then she found a little note fastened to the pretty hand, and read:

> "Dear little mother, take me in:
> I will do my best your heart to win.
> I've the realest hair and a lasting bloom,
> And you'll find my trunk, with yours, in your room."

And, sure enough, when Milly rushed up stairs to see, there was a miniature Saratoga trunk containing everything the heart of doll could wish; and when she came quite to the bottom she found two visiting-cards: "Mr. George Loring" and "Mr. John Loring."

"I might have guessed that it was Uncle George and Uncle

Jack," she cried rapturously.—" Oh, come with me right away, you beauty, till I thank them all." .

If any stranger had been in the parlor, I am afraid he would have thought that a very crazy little girl lived in that house ; but, fortunately, nobody was there who did not know all about it. Milly's home-presents had been on the breakfast-table—a charming story-book and a beautifully-fitted work-box—and this shower of fairy-gifts had taken her entirely by surprise. When the excitement had subsided a little, Milly suddenly found herself very hungry, and remembered that she had not waited to eat much breakfast. But when she modestly asked for a roll, Aunt Mary said, smiling, "I think I remember Somebody used to have a great liking for Huldah's mush, and I have no doubt there will be enough left to fry for breakfast if you eat a bowlful now."

So Milly ran into the kitchen, and Huldah poured rich milk over the steaming mush, and Milly made a table of the little bench which Huldah pulled out for her to sit on, but Rover and Douglas and the black cat, and the small kitten who had not a name yet, all watched her so wistfully that she left half her generous portion to divide among them, although Huldah declared, indignantly, that they had all had as much breakfast as ever they could eat.

And then little Hatty came, and the two children, after exchanging very loving greetings, wandered off hand in hand. There was so much to see and to do—ferns and flowers to gather to adorn

the birthday tea-table, the beach to visit, the new swing and hammock to try, the lovely waxen lady with her pretty wardrobe to be exhibited and admired—no wonder the time flew and both little maidens were surprised by the ringing of the dinner-bell before anything had been done besides the visit to the barn and the longer visit to the doll and her trunk.

"I shall call her Harriet Helen," said Milly as she and Nelly tripped down to dinner; and Hatty acknowledged her share of the honor with a very loving kiss.

Dinner at Sweetbrier Farm took place at the good old-fashioned hour of one o'clock, so there was time for a little rest in the hazel bower before the walk to the beach; and then the little maids started out once more, to return laden with treasures—maidenhair fern, and great white daisies with golden hearts, and wild honeysuckle, and curious shells and stones picked up on the beach. And while they were adorning the table, which was set in the wide, vine-covered back piazza, Nelly came and helped and admired. Old Speckle's contribution to the feast was skilfully scrambled by Huldah; the cream cheese and the pretty cake had each a wreath of ferns and daisies; there was a great dish of early strawberries, coaxed into ripeness by the care of the two uncles for this wonderful day—such cream and milk and butter and sweet homemade bread and crisp lettuce and radishes as poor city people do not even dream of.

And then, when the birthday-feast had been duly honored, the two uncles carried off the children to help them "call the cattle home;" and Milly nearly jumped into the brook in her haste to reach old Spot, who stood on the other side with a nearly grown-up calf of her very own.

And then they wandered home in the soft summer twilight, and a great round moon came up from behind the hills and shone on the snowy fleeces of the sheep as they lay scattered over the tranquil meadow. And when the little friends had said good-night, and gone home through the moonlit fields with their father, who had come for them, Milly said that she was so "tired with happiness"

"OLD SPOT STOOD ON THE OTHER SIDE WITH HER CALF."

that she would go to bed; so, first undressing her new child, and then herself, she sank with a happy sigh into her white nest. But before she had even begun to go to sleep she heard under her window the tinkle of a guitar.

"It's Uncle John!" she said, springing up and peeping from the window; "and oh, I haven't heard him play and sing for nearly a year, and I've never in my whole life been serenaded before!"

But could that romantic-looking minstrel, in a Spanish-looking hat and cloak and with the ribbon of his guitar thrown over his shoulder, be quiet Uncle John? Milly doubted for a minute, but when the sweet tenor voice joined the accompaniment of the guitar she smiled to herself: "It *is* Uncle John; he can't disguise his voice. And when he is done I will throw him a flower; they always do that in stories."

Perhaps it was not a usual selection for a serenade, but this was what the minstrel sang:

"Sleep, baby, sleep!
Thy father's watching the sheep,
Thy mother's shaking the Dreamland tree,
And down drops a little dream for thee:
Sleep, baby, sleep!

"Sleep, baby, sleep!
The large stars are the sheep,
The little stars are the lambs, I guess;
The bright moon is the shepherdess:
Sleep, baby, sleep!

"Sleep, baby, sleep!
And cry not like a sheep,
Else the sheep-dog will bark and whine,
And bite this naughty child of mine:
Sleep, baby, sleep!

"Sleep, baby, sleep!
    Thy Saviour loves his sheep:
He is the Lamb of God on high,
Who for our sakes came down to die:
    Sleep, baby, sleep!

"Sleep, baby, sleep!
    Away to tend the sheep—
Away, thou sheep-dog fierce and wild,
And do not harm my sleeping child!
    Sleep, baby, sleep!"

And as the last note died away a sweet white rose fell on the troubadour's guitar. He kissed his hand to his little lady, and she fell asleep with sweet fragments of his song drifting through her mind as the white clouds were drifting over the silver face of the moon.

THE KING'S THREE SONS.

IT was a smiling and peaceful kingdom, truly,
    And the King of Gingal was every inch a king;
So his sons, for wilfully breaking a law made newly,
    Were turned out of doors because they would not sing.
After deep thought had this strange law been spoken,
    For deep in his heart the good of his people lay:
"By none who love me," he said, "will this law be broken;
    Each of my subjects must sing at least once a day."

Moodily strode the eldest son one morning
    Forth from the palace, angry and ashamed,
Muttering, "I gave my royal father warning:
    I cannot help it; why should I be blamed?
How can I sing, seeing, as I do daily,
    Right slain or wounded by the touch of wrong?
The innocent suffer; guilty ones go gayly;
    My heart is all too hot and wroth for song."

On the next day went mournfully another,
    His gentle face marred by a look of sadness.
"Alas!" he said, "I cannot blame my brother;
    While pain has victims where is room for gladness?
In the dark forest found I, as I wandered,
    A wounded stag, a bird with broken wing;
As on this helpless suffering I pondered,
    How thought my royal father I could sing?"

On the third day a third son left the palace,
    And rushed to hide his anger in the wood.
"This law," he said, "is nothing but sheer malice:
    Why am I never to be understood?
When deep research and lofty thought enchain me,
    Shall I break off a foolish song to sing?
Surely this law was only framed to pain me:
    It was not well done of my lord the king."

The eldest son, whom want or care had never
    Before come near, stood at a cottage-door
Asking for shelter; "And I will endeavor
    To work for you," he faltered.—" Say no more,"
The cotter cried: his voice was clear and ringing;
    He gave his hand with frank and smiling grace.

"EACH OF MY SUBJECTS MUST SING AT LEAST ONCE A DAY."

See Page 114

"At dusk," he said, "all comers find me singing:
  It guides full many a wanderer to the place.

"You wonder why I sing? You see the token
  That once I lived not humbly? It is true;
But from the life I thought for ever broken
  A higher, better life has sprung anew.

"HER BREAST AGAINST A THORN, THE NIGHTINGALE."

Here have I watched sweet growths from death upspringing;
  Hope is fulfilled, it may be soon or late.
Good cause have I, forsooth, my friend, for singing,
  For I have learned the lesson, Trust and Wait."

The gentle boy, whom pity had so saddened,
  Sank down in weariness beneath an oak:

A gush of music near his whole heart gladdened,
    The while with tenderness it almost broke.
"Ah, could I sing that song!" he murmured, seeking
    To find the singer of the enchanted vale.
And he discovered, even as he was speaking,
    Her breast against a thorn, the nightingale.

"I let the thorns that pierced me hush my singing,"
    He said with shame; and then the woods again
With the full melody of the bird were ringing,
    Who used her pain to learn to comfort pain.
"I will go back; I have been weak, defying
    A law whose worth I did not understand.
Now shall my father find, in my complying,
    That full obedience love should e'er command."

The third son found no shelter; in the forest,
    Stretched on dead leaves, he lay the whole night long,
And when the darkness and the chill were sorest,
    The dawn broke, and he heard the lark's glad song.
His dim eyes followed, up through the blue unbroken
    By cloud or mist, the singer in her flight,
Until her glad song was the only token
    That she had reached that far, untroubled height.

DEER IN THE FOREST. See Page 116.

And then the wayward prince upstarted, sobbing :
  "My father, it was I who did the wrong!
Selfishly have I lived, yet have been robbing
  Myself of joy in grudging thee the song."
With hasty step he sought his home ; the others
  By different roads met him without the gate :
Joyful the greeting was between the brothers,
  Who entered, singing, "It is not too late!"

My little children, you whose lives of gladness,
  Unshadowed yet, make singing seem like speech,
Treasure your songs up for the times of sadness
  Which on your way will surely come to each.
It will be hard sometimes. We live forgetting,
  Too often, that we are children of a King :
Life brings us toiling, mourning, waiting, fretting ;
  Out of it all look up, dear hearts, and sing!

TWO GOOD FRIENDS.

"YES," purred the Black Cat, in a loud, musical purr, "her face, her sweet young face, is the very first thing which I distinctly remember, although, of course, I must have seen other things first. I climbed in, with great difficulty, over the sill of a low window, and there she sat, in a white gown and with a bow of blue ribbon in her soft brown hair. She had a great bunch of sewing in her lap, but she threw it down and picked me up, and cuddled me and loved me and talked to me, until I made up my mind that I would be civil to the rest, but would belong only to her. And I have done it ever since. They all like me—I hear something pleasant said about me every day by one or the other

"I HAVE A GOOD BED BY THE KITCHEN-FIRE."

of them—but Clementine is the only one who tells me things when we are quite alone. It must have been in the summer, that first day that she picked me up. The trees were full of leaves, and the air was full of birds, and the passion-vine was blooming all over the window. But winter is just as good. We have warm red curtains and cushions in winter, and beautiful bright fires which heat one's back delightfully, and Clementine sits with me more in winter, especially in the evenings."

"You have a very happy home, my dear," purred the White Cat gently—" far happier than I have ever had. They give me enough to eat at my house, and a good bed by the kitchen-fire, and they like to see me clean and neat, and they praise me whenever I catch a rat or mouse; but nobody ever picks me up and cuddles me, and once, when I was feeling very lonely and jumped up in the housekeeper's lap, she held up both hands and stood up in a way which slid me off. I suppose I must have looked hurt—I felt so—for she said good-naturedly, 'There, Pussy, you're a good little cat, but your place is the floor. I can't have your hairs all over my gown;' and then she turned to the housemaid, and said, 'I don't know why it is, but it always gives me a kind of cold creep down my back to touch a cat.'

"I walked round behind her at once; I didn't see anything of the cold creep, or I would have caught it for her; but you may well believe that I have never sat on her lap since, and that I have hesitated about trying any one else."

The White Cat, whose family had moved into the neighborhood recently, was taking tea with the Black Cat, whose family had lived for many, many years in the beautiful old gabled house among the trees. They were sitting in front of a cheerful fire, and it seemed to them all the cozier as they listened to the wind among the trees and the sleet dashing against the windows. The warm red curtains were closely drawn. A softly burning lamp stood among many books on the little table, and on the red couch drawn up to one side of the fire lay Clementine asleep.

"THEY WERE SITTING IN FRONT OF A CHEERFUL FIRE."

"I'm afraid she isn't well," purred the Black Cat softly, and looking a little anxiously at the pretty sleeping face, which seemed flushed. "She *would* go out this afternoon in all the storm, because she had promised some things to some of her poor people. I wish you could have seen her when she came in: her cheeks were as red as roses, and the wind had pulled her hair all about her eyes. But she was all out of breath, and very wet indeed, and as she went to change her clothes and shoes, the housemaid—who is a careless young thing—stopped her to tell her about some sick person who had sent for beef-tea; and she stopped to weigh the beef and measure the water; and when she came up to her room at last her cheeks were quite white and she was shivering. If her mother had only been at home, she would have given Clementine some hot tea and made her go to bed; but there was the bread-and-butter to cut, and the tea to pour out for her father and the children; so she ran down again when she had changed her clothes and shoes: she never seems to remember that she has a herself."

"I think we grow like the people with whom we live," purred the White Cat. "I feel myself growing more reserved and quiet every day, although I try to be cheerful and playful with my baby, for I don't wish *her* to grow up silent and sad.—But you have quite forgotten that I came over this evening expressly to hear you tell about the flood, and how you saved Clementine's little brother."

"I CARRIED HER TO THE SOFT MAT."

"Oh," purred the Black Cat modestly, "very probably the baby would have been saved without me—no doubt some one would have seen the cradle. But tell me, first, about *your* baby: you know I haven't seen her yet. Don't they take any notice of *her?*"

"About as much as they do of me," purred the White Cat sadly. "And I really made an effort for her sake—a very great effort for me. I thought perhaps their hearts would be touched by her sweet little ways, so I carried her to the soft mat in front of the younger sister's door, and stood there till the door opened and she came out. She was not cross—she never is—but she called the housemaid and said, 'Carry the kitten back to its basket, Jane; and if you see the cat bringing it here again, just shut them in the laundry, and leave a window open for the cat to go in and out.' That is what they all call me—'the cat,' or 'Pussy,' or 'Kitty.' They have never even given me a name!" and the White Cat put her paw over her eyes for a minute.

"That *is* hard," purred the Black Cat feelingly, "but perhaps they don't know any better. I always try to think that is the reason when people treat me as I don't like to be treated, for I am certain I have often annoyed others in that way myself."

"Perhaps you are right," purred the White Cat, brightening up a little; "I didn't think of that before. But now do tell me about the flood; I must be going soon: I haven't ever left my baby this long before."

"It was several years ago," purred the Black Cat thoughtfully— "I don't know just how many, for I never could learn to count, but I was not quite grown up. It rained for days and days, almost without stopping a minute, and one night, just before bedtime, Clementine's father came in and said, 'I don't like the look of the river; it is nearly up to the lower terrace, and rising rapidly.'

"'It came a little higher than that last spring, dear,' said Clementine's mother, ' but it didn't do any damage, and we'll hope it will not this time.'

"So they went to bed, but I did not. I had that uneasy feeling which comes over me when I am anywhere near where mice are hidden. They always left the doors of the rooms open at night, and after the lights were put out I just walked softly from room to room, so that I might be ready to wake them in case anything should happen. Several of the bedrooms were on the ground-floor—Clementine's, and her mother's and father's, and a little room between where the nurse and Baby slept. I heard the water running faster and faster, and at last, when I crossed the hall, I found the floor was wet, and there was a noise, as if people were knocking at the great front doors of the hall. I thought it was high time to wake my people up, and that I had better wake the father first, because he was the oldest and strongest, and would know best what to do.

"But before I could get out of the hall the front and back doors burst open at once with a noise like loud thunder; the water rushed in as if the whole river were coming, and I was lifted off my feet as if I had been a feather and swept out of the front door. I managed to seize a chair and cling desperately to it, and I had only floated along for a few minutes when I heard the baby cry. It was not very dark, for there was a large moon behind the clouds, and it had stopped raining; so in a few minutes I could see the cradle quite plainly. It was floating very nicely, just like a boat,

"THE BABY WAKED AND PLAYED WITH HIS FINGERS."

See Page 93.

and I decided at once that it was my duty to join the baby; he might stop crying, and then float silently away before any one knew where he was. I could easily have jumped to the cradle, but I was afraid that my weight, added so suddenly, might make it rock, and so fill it; so I left my chair, and with great difficulty struggled through the water and climbed carefully in over the foot-board. And, sure enough, the baby did stop crying in a few minutes, and went to sleep. I don't know how many hours it was before they found us. We had floated quite away from our home, and I knew by the barns and stacks that we must be in a farmyard, but I could not see any one anywhere, and so I kept quiet, saving up all my mews till I should have a chance to make some one hear.

"I did not have to wait much longer. The baby waked and lay quite still, playing with his fingers and staring about with great, wondering eyes. And then I saw a boat away off, around the corner of a barn, and I knew my time had come to mew. I don't think I ever made such a noise in my life as I did then—no, not even on the few occasions when my tail had been stepped upon. And they heard me; I soon saw the boat turn and come toward us, and then I saw that the two people in it were Baby's mother and father. The poor mother sat with clasped hands as the father poled the boat along with all his might, and in a few minutes they had come up close to the cradle and lifted out their baby, and me too. Then they tied the cradle to the end of the boat, and we all went to a house where the water had not come in, and stayed till the river went down and our own house was dry and clean once more; and it was after this that the father had that beautiful broad-topped wall, where you and I so often meet, built all along the front of our place, and banked up behind with earth almost to the top."

"That was *very* interesting," purred the White Cat as the Black Cat stopped. "No wonder they all love you and make so much of you. I wish such an opportunity would come to me; it might change everything. But I really must go now: I had no idea of staying so late, and I don't know what might happen if my baby were to cry much: they might give her away to somebody. Good-night, and thank you for a very pleasant evening;" and the White Cat was gone.

The Black Cat turned and looked at Clementine. "Her cheeks are as red as they were when she came in this afternoon," she purred, "so perhaps she will not be ill, after all."

It was a bright afternoon nearly a week after this pleasant evening, and the Black Cat was sitting on top of the wall in the sun; but she looked very serious, and took no notice of the dead leaves which blew about, nor of the birds which hopped along the bank looking for worms; she did not even see that the White Cat was coming until their noses almost touched, and then she started up, exclaiming, "Bless me! how you made me jump!"

"I beg your pardon," purred the White Cat meekly, "but I

thought you must see me. I'm afraid something is the matter, you look so sad."

"There is, indeed," purred the Black Cat. "Clementine is ill, very ill. It began that evening you took tea with me, as, you know, we feared that it would; and now she has something with a hard name: I couldn't quite make it out, although I heard the doctor tell her mother, but I am pretty sure he said it was something 'new.' I sat outside the door listening until I found that I was in the way, and her breathing sounded like mine did once when they accidentally put a feather bed on top of me. They sent for her mother right away, and everybody is keeping very still; even the baby does not scream when he is washed, and I heard him saying to himself, 'Poor Tiny!' It went to my very heart." And the Black Cat covered her eyes with her paw.

"Don't give way, my dear friend," purred the White Cat, soothingly. "Clementine is very young, and I think that helps people to get well. And our Miss Abigail was ill for weeks, and they all cried and said she couldn't get well, possibly; but I do believe she is stronger now than the other two. And, somehow, it seems to me that the way you all love Clementine will keep her from dying."

"You are a real comforter," purred the Black Cat, bracing up, "and I will try to feel more hopeful. But what has made you so much brighter? You look like another cat."

"And I feel like one," purred the White Cat cheerfully. "Since

I saw you last a little child has come to live with us, and you can't imagine the difference it has made already. She is a timid little thing, and at first the great silent house and the quiet old ladies made her look just as I felt; so I thought perhaps it would cheer her up a little if she could see my baby; she looked so quiet and gentle that I was not afraid to trust her. She had been sent out to play in the yard, and the cook—who is always afraid we will not get enough to eat—called her in and gave her a nice bowl of bread and cream. I waited till she had finished it, for I did not wish her to think that I was begging, and then I came and told her about the kitten. She was a little afraid at first—she is so *very* small—but I smiled and purred, and presently she said softly, 'Poor pussy! Why didn't you come sooner? You should have had some, but now it is all gone.' I soon made her see that I wished her to follow me; and I would like you to have seen her when she found the kitten. She has been as gay as a lark ever since, and the old aunts are so pleased with the

"I CAME AND TOLD HER ABOUT THE KITTEN."

change that they encourage her to play with it; they have actually given her a little basket with a cushion in it to carry the kitten about, so that she may not handle it too much. And the dear little thing has named us both, and insists upon having us called by our names. She calls me Lily, and the baby Blossom, and you may be sure that I come the very moment I hear my name. It all seems too good to be true."

"I congratulate you heartily," purred the Black Cat, giving her paw to the White Cat. "But I really must run in now; it is about time for the doctor's visit, and I wish to hear what he says to-day. I'll be here again to-morrow morning if the weather is good, and tell you. Good-bye."

"Oh, thank you," purred the White Cat. "I was going to ask you to let me know, I feel so interested. I'll be sure to be here. Good-bye."

And the White Cat trotted back to her baby and their new friend, while the Black Cat stole silently up to Clementine's door to wait for the coming of the doctor.

By and by Clementine's mother came out of the room, and when she saw the Black Cat she stopped and stroked him. "Poor Douglas!" she said softly; "I do believe you know, for you love Clementine better than any of the rest of us, and she petted you so much that I think you must miss her. She is very ill, but it seems to me that she is just a little, little bit better to-day; and if the doctor should think so too, you shall see her for a few minutes this evening. But you must keep quite still, and not try to make her speak to you, for even that much excitement might do her harm." And, stroking Douglas again, Clementine's mother went down stairs to wait for the doctor.

It rained a little the next morning, but the two friends met on the wall notwithstanding.

"I was so anxious to hear how Clementine was that I thought I'd come on the chance of *your* coming," purred the White Cat when they had exchanged "good-mornings."

"I somehow thought you would be here," purred the Black Cat, "and I don't mind a little wetting now and then: it obliges one to give one's self such a thorough good licking afterward that it is good for one's coat. She's better—the mother thought so first, and the doctor said so when he came—and I've seen her! I'm thankful they told me she was better before I saw her, for I never should have thought so to look at her. I could only stay a minute, and was obliged to keep very still. Her mother told me about it in the morning, just after I saw you, but she did not take me in till just at sunset, because Clementine was asleep then, as she explained to me. She looked ever so much smaller, and her poor little face and hands were as white as the pillow-case. I was almost afraid, for a minute, that she was dead, but then I saw that she was breathing very softly and regularly. There was a bunch of white roses on the window-sill from the bush she loves so much, but she really looked whiter than they did. Still, the family seems very hopeful about her, and I know they can tell better than I can; so I have made up my mind to believe them, and her mother has prom-

"CLEMENTINE WAS ASLEEP."

ised that I shall see her again to-morrow for a few minutes when she is awake."

"That is good news indeed," purred the White Cat, looking very much relieved; "and I have something to tell you too. I have made another friend. You know we all like a ramble in the fields and woods sometimes, and I was out for one yesterday afternoon: nobody could be better fed than I am, but once in a while I take a fancy for something I have caught myself, and I did think yesterday that I would like a bird. I wanted a mouse too, for it is high time for me to begin teaching Blossom, and field-mice are better for practice than house-mice. So I went across the large field to the wood. I was just climbing a fence when I saw a very fine-looking gray cat coming toward me. I have met him several times in the neighborhood lately, but we had never been introduced, so I had not spoken. He was evidently hunting too, and almost under his feet, crouching among the leaves, was a snipe which he was passing directly by. Of course I called to him, and he caught the snipe without any trouble, but he insisted upon my accepting it, because, he said, he should not have caught it if I had not happened to see it. He carried it home for me, and was most entertaining all the way. He had heard of your exploit, and he asks your permission to call."

"I shall be very happy to see him," purred the Black Cat, graciously, "but I would rather he should wait for a few days, until I feel quite easy about Clementine. You might bring him some day next week."

"Very well," purred the White Cat; "I'll tell him the first time I see him again. And now I must go. Be here to-morrow morning if you can, for I shall want to hear about Clementine."

"She spoke to me!" purred the Black Cat joyfully the next

"ALMOST UNDER HIS FEET WAS A SNIPE."

morning as soon as he was near enough to the White Cat to make her hear. "She asked to have me put on the bed, and I was there nearly all the morning. Every little while she would stroke my head and talk to me, and to-morrow she is to sit up."

"I am just as glad as I can be," purred the White Cat, delightedly, "and as soon as she is down stairs I wish you would take me in to see her: I feel as if I must know her after hearing so much about her."

"I will, with pleasure," purred the Black Cat, "and if the Gray Cat should turn out a desirable acquaintance, we will take him too. Clementine is very fond of cats, and no doubt it would please her to meet a new one."

So now *you* understand how it was, but you cannot imagine Clementine's astonishment, the first day that her reclining-chair was wheeled out upon the piazza, when a solemn procession of three cats, Black, White, and Gray, marched up the walk and sat down in front of her chair. The Black Cat tried to make her understand that he had brought the other two to call on her. I am afraid he did not quite succeed, but she was very polite and sent for some cream for them, and they went away quite satisfied. And when she was well again, and could walk once more about the old garden, she was often joined by one or other of them, and sometimes by all three.

TWO WAYS.

VERY gloomy-faced little dog was Mopsy as he sat in the door of his kennel one frosty morning and watched the sparrows holding high festival over the breakfast he had scornfully and without any thanks declined. He was in disgrace, he was separated from his beloved Polly, and, for the first time in six months or more, he was chained. He—the little petted dog, who had his own special stool by the fire, his own blue china dish on the zinc behind the stove, his own little feather bed in a corner of Polly's room— had been carried out by the tall waiter, in spite of indignant growls and howls, and chained to an old kennel in front of the coach-house! He would not admit to himself that he had first behaved very badly indeed. No; he was keeping himself angry by growling to the sparrows: "What did Polly mean, then, by taking in that cur, and expecting me to treat him as if he were my equal? It would have been bad enough if he had been a decent, well-bred dog; even then Polly would have been giving him half the love that belongs to me. But a creature like that—a mongrel, a dog who does not even bark grammatically, who makes an unpleasant noise when he eats, and licks his plate when he has finished as if

he never expected to have another good meal,—it is intolerable! And such a fuss as they all made over him just because he had had a tin kettle tied to his tail and been chased a little! I dare say he would have bitten the string in two if Polly had not cut it, and the manner in which he dashed into our grounds from the road was highly impertinent—howling, too, at the top of his voice! It would have served him no more than right if he had been shot for a mad dog. But no; they must all go on their knees, Polly and Tom and the cook and Nurse, and even master and mistress; and it was, 'Oh, the *poor* little dog!' 'Oh, the *dear* little dog!' till I was perfectly sick of hearing them. Little, indeed! He's ever so much longer than I am, if he is narrower. And if they think chaining me up in this wicked, barbarous fashion will make me civil to him, they are vastly mistaken, that's all. No; I shall just stay here, and not eat anything, and pine away and die; *then* they will be filled with remorse. And if that cur doesn't want his ugly head taken off, he'd better keep out of my way."

Now, this was Mopsy's view of it. The real truth was, that he had behaved shockingly. The "cur," as he called him, but whom Polly had named "Stray," had merely attempted to finish the breakfast which Mopsy had left and did not want at all. Polly had filled both their plates with mush and milk before she would sit down to her own breakfast, and Mopsy, who smelt mutton-chops, had eaten a few mouthfuls of his and then turned away with a sniff, while poor Stray, to whom plenty to eat was a novelty and a luxury, had thought it a breakfast fit for the king of dogs, and, having licked his own plate clean, had quietly begun on Mopsy's despised breakfast. Mopsy was a spoiled little dog—there was no mistake about that—and he flew at the stranger savagely, and, being stronger and heavier, through good care and feeding, than the other was, he soon had him howling on the floor, while he, Mopsy, stood over him, giving him a savage nip whenever he tried to get up.

Polly, who always took the part of the oppressed even when she loved the oppressor, turned with a great deal of dignity to Jenks, the tall waiter, and said, "Jenks, you will please carry Mopsy out to the dog-house, and put some clean straw in it, and fasten his collar to the chain. I will let him loose again when he promises to behave properly to poor Stray."

So Jenks, not without some fear of being snapped at, gathered Mopsy up in his long arms and did as his little mistress requested; and Mopsy was so breathless with astonishment and indignation that it never occurred to him, until after he was chained and by himself, that he might have nipped Jenks too. It would have been the basest ingratitude, for Jenks was a very patient man, and always did what was politely asked of him. He had even helped Polly to wash Stray, or rather had washed him while Polly looked on and thought she was helping, and had kindly said that "when the poor misused beast fattened up a bit he wouldn't be a bad-looking dog, and might be trained to follow the carriage."

This had greatly delighted Polly, as kind-hearted Jenks knew it

"POLLY LIKED IRONING. AND SHE DID IT WITH ALL HER MIGHT."

See Page 149

would. Mopsy always went in Polly's lap when the family took a drive, so that the new dog would not be interfering with his privileges by following the carriage. Polly invested fifteen cents in a blue soup-plate for the new dog; it was only "willow-ware," and Mopsy's was real china. "So you see, papa," Polly argued, "Mopsy can't possibly be jealous, and yet this willow-ware plate must be so much better than anything poor Stray has had before that *he* will be quite pleased."

So you may judge of Polly's disappointment and indignation when Mopsy first refused to say a friendly word to the new dog, and then flew at him in the disgraceful manner of which I have just told you.

It was holiday-t'me, so there was no school to divert Polly's mind from her pet's bad behavior.

"What would you do, Nurse, if you were me this morning?" she asked, a little disconsolately, after breakfast.

"I think I'd have a family-wash, deary," said Nurse gravely. "I've noticed that nearly all your children's clothes are in the basket, and you couldn't have a better day for drying."

"That's the very thing!" said Polly joyfully; and forthwith the playroom was rummaged for every garment and sheet and pillow-case and table-cloth belonging to Polly's family of eight, and by the time the last "piece" was hung out the first ones were dry and ready for sprinkling; and the ironing was not begun until after the early dinner, so large was the wash that week. Polly liked ironing; she "bore on" hard, and smoothed out the pieces first with her fingers, and did it, as she did most things, with all her might; so for a little while she was seriously happy over her ironing-table, and almost forgot the sad affair of the morning.

Meanwhile, Stray was nearly as unhappy as Mopsy was. He had, without in the least intending it, brought discord into a family which had shown him more kindness than he had before experienced in his short and miserable life. He went as near Mopsy's prison as he dared, to be greeted by savage growls. Then he wandered disconsolately about the grounds, trying to make up his mind to run away and be once more a vagabond upon the face of the earth.

"I should be no worse off than I was before these lovely people took me in," he argued with himself; "in fact, I should be better off, for although I am still thin, I don't look starved any more, and I am nice and clean now. If I can only manage to sit up on my hind legs, as Mopsy does, and beg at kitchen-doors, I think I can pick up enough to keep me from starving. But oh, it is so pleasant to have a real home and to be petted and spoken to gently! How can I go away from it all when I have never had it before?"

He loitered back to the neighborhood of the coach-house, and, in spite of his trouble, became very much interested in watching Polly's ducks. There was a family of four funny little yellow ducklings, and two of them had taken hold of opposite ends of a long, fat worm. They pulled and tugged: neither would let go; and the poor worm, being tough, did not settle the difficulty by coming in two.

"THEY PULLED AND TUGGED, AND NEITHER WOULD LET GO."

Finally, when both ducklings were out of breath with the struggle, one let go his hold long enough to say, "I found it first. You just give it to me now!"

And the other one, not stopping to think, opened his bill and said, "I saw it as soon as you did. *You* just give it to *me!*"

And while they were saying this the worm very wisely slipped into a convenient hole, and when they looked down for him he wasn't there!

Both ducklings looked excessively foolish. Then one sidled up to the other, and said meekly, "I'm sorry: let's be friends."

"So am I: let's," said the other; and then they both went to work together to dig out the worm, and when they found him they divided him equally between them.

"Ah," said the poor dog to himself, sorrowfully, "if only Mopsy would come to an agreement like that, how pleasant it would be!"

He wandered into the stable, for he felt a great admiration for the beautiful gray horse with his kind eyes and gracefully-arched neck, and he thought, "If I could only screw up my courage to consult him about it—he looks so wise—I've no doubt *he* could think of some way in which I could win Mopsy over to be at least civil to me."

Puck, the large gray cat, who was very intimate with Prince, the horse, was walking round the edge of Prince's watering-trough— which was not a common trough at all, but a round marble basin— rubbing against his nose every time she came round to where it was, while he looked gently down at his small friend. They did not see poor Stray, who lay meekly down under the manger, and they went on talking.

"PUCK, THE CAT, WAS WALKING ROUND PRINCE'S WATERING-TROUGH."

See page 152.

"It seems so strange to me now," said Puck, "that I did not like you at first. I feel ashamed whenever I think about how cross and ugly I was, and how I would have scratched you if I only had not been afraid. And I put up my back and hissed at you every time I came near you, but you always smiled down at me so kindly that after a while I began to think I must be a very bad-tempered cat; and then I felt as if I would like to be friends with you, but I was afraid you would not wish to be, after the dreadful way in which I had behaved; and you don't know how I trembled that first time I jumped up on the manger and begged your pardon. And you were so good to me—then and ever since—you dear, beautiful, good-tempered horse!"

"I knew you could be conquered by kindness," said Prince gently; "I never met any one yet who could not;" and he rubbed Puck's head with his nice soft nose.

Stray walked out of the stable quite cheerfully. "There is no use in my bothering Mr. Prince," he said to himself. "I know what to do now, and I'll do it. Perhaps then I need not leave this lovely new home; surely there is room enough in it, and in dear little Miss Polly's warm heart, for both Mopsy and me."

So, patiently and cheerfully, day after day, Stray went as near Mopsy's prison as he dared, and offered to run errands for Mopsy, to sit and talk with him, to bring him all the best bones that he himself should have given to him; in short, to do anything whatever that Mopsy could think of. At first, Mopsy only growled, and when

Polly came to visit him and cry over him, as she did two or three times every day, he was sullenly silent. But little by little he grew ashamed. The poor patient dog's wistful, loving face, Polly's affectionate reproaches and assurances that she could love another dog without unloving him, were having their effect; and one day, when Polly came to have a talk with him, she found, to her great joy, the two dogs sitting close together, engaged in friendly conversation.

At once the chain was loosed from Mopsy's collar, and he and Stray went bounding before her to the house. And when supper-time came, Mopsy proved the sincerity of his repentance by insisting that Stray should eat his supper out of the blue china dish, while he, Mopsy, ate his from the willow-ware.

"And now," said Polly joyously when the early supper was over, "we will have our concert again.—Come, sister, come, Baby, come, Mopsy, and let Stray hear you sing."

The joke was, that the baby and Mopsy both thought they could sing. So, while the older sister played a little tune on the piano, the baby, seated on a stool, and Mopsy, perched up in the great arm-chair, each warbled, greatly to his own satisfaction, as long as the sister would play.

And Stray, who had not a jealous bone in his body, sat listening with open mouth and a look in his eyes which seemed to say, "How beautiful! how touching! What a genius is here!"

And Polly and her father, standing behind the group, where they could see it all, laughed until they nearly cried.

"THE BABY, SEATED ON A STOOL, AND MOPSY, IN A CHAIR, EACH SANG."
See Page 136

THE MAY-QUEEN.

COME, little children, come away,
Follow your queen, the Queen of May,
  Where the young leaves are spring-
    ing;
Crown her with flowers, raise her throne
Here where the grass has greenest grown—
  Here, where the birds are singing.

Hail her with merry song and shout—
Never a cross word, never a pout,
  Come into all your playing.
Songs like the singing of the birds,
Happiest laughter and loving words,
  Take as you go a-Maying.

Winter is over, storm and cloud,
Blustering March winds rude and loud,
  Showers that spoil the play-time.

"SCEPTRE AND TRAIN TO GRACE YOUR QUEEN."

Where was so lately snow and sleet,
Bright little crocuses, violets sweet,
Tell of the happy May-time.

Sceptre and train to grace your Queen—
Happiest monarch ever seen,
  Reigning for one bright play-day:

"SEEK FOR YOUR QUEEN WHERE HIDDEN LIE."

Flowers to strew along her way—
'Surely the little Queen must say,
  "Never was fairer May Day."

Seek for your Queen where hidden lie
Beds of arbutus, pure and shy,
  Fit for a May Queen's bowers.
It is so sweet, the gentle wind
Helps you its hiding-place to find,
  Fairest of all May flowers.

Gather the sweetness as you go ;
Store it within your hearts, and so
  Keep every moment's pleasure ;
Then, when the winter comes, this day
Shall be for the merry Queen of May
  And each of her maids a treasure.

MRS. CLUCK'S CHILDREN.

MRS. CLUCK was a very careful mother: so careful and so much to be depended upon was she that the farmer's wife always gave her the best eggs and the ones which she was most anxious to have hatched. You will think, perhaps, that this made her vain, but it did not at all; she grew more and more anxious as she found how much was expected of her, and whenever she had a brood of young chickens nearly fretted and scolded her feathers off. So you may think what a state of mind she was in last spring when out of a "setting" of fifteen eggs—eggs for which the farmer's wife had sent a long way and paid a high price, as she took care to tell poor Mrs. Cluck when she set her on them—only twelve hatched. Perhaps you will think that this was doing pretty well; and so it would have been for an ordinary hen, but not for Mrs. Cluck. You see, the price of being famous is being obliged to live up to one's character or else suffer the mortification of being considered a failure.

The misfortune of wasting three high-priced eggs so affected Mrs. Cluck's temper that this particular brood of chickens had a hard time of it. They were scolded and screamed at if they ventured two feet away from their mother, until the meek ones drooped and the high-spirited ones answered back; and one very impertinent little cock, who thought he knew pretty much everything, adopted the plan of standing on her back and tickling her through her feathers.

"I'm up here, all safe," he would say, making a face at the others as he spoke.

This was bad enough, but I really think one of the little hens was worse. She lost all spirit and what little sense she had, and used to sit about with her mouth wide open, looking as if she had never had an idea in her head.

Somehow, this seemed to exasperate Mrs. Cluck more than all the impudence of the little cock, and she even threatened that she would tie up the poor little hen's head to make her keep her mouth shut.

Things were in this unpleasant state when it was announced in the chicken-yard that a very fine young cock was coming to give crowing-lessons. All the little cocks in Mrs. Cluck's family crowded round her, clamoring, "Oh, mother, may we take lessons? Oh, do *please* let us! The old cock here has such a dreadfully old-fashioned crow!"

"Indeed, you may not," said Mrs. Cluck, crossly. "I can't leave your sisters alone while I take you to any crowing-lessons. There's a rumor of a weazel being somewhere about, and I saw a hawk

"ONE VERY IMPERTINENT LITTLE COCK STOOD ON HER BACK."

myself only yesterday. You'll learn to crow fast enough, without any teaching."

The little cocks looked very sulky, all but the impudent one: he merely looked thoughtful.

And the next morning, when the young cock came to the stone on which he was going to stand to give his lessons, he found five ridiculous little chickens with scarcely a pin-feather apiece, and one little yellow duckling. And the best of the joke was, that one of the five chickens was the poor little silly hen! The bad little cock, who had come without leave or license, had wanted somebody to share the blame with him when he went back to his mother, and he had persuaded his sister that there was no reason why a hen should not learn to crow as well as any rooster.

The professor of crowing was not at all pleased either with the size of his class or the age of his scholars, but he was a cock of his word; so he gave them a good hour's instruction, only being careful to ascertain before he began that they had each brought him the fee agreed upon—a fine fat worm or a dozen kernels of corn. He told the yellow duckling, honestly, that it was quite impossible that she should ever learn to crow, and that he would advise her not to join the class; but she scratched her head and said she didn't see why, and was so angry about it that he said it was no concern of his, and let her stay. Of course, *she* did not learn to crow, but, if you will believe it, that poor little hen did! Whether it was because her mouth was already open when the lesson began, or because she did exactly what the professor

"THE PROFESSOR OF CROWING GAVE THEM AN HOUR'S LESSON"

See Page 160

told her, I don't know, but she actually crowed better when the lesson was over than any of the little cocks.

And when she and her naughty brother reached home, and she, thinking to please her mother with her new accomplishment, burst out with a weak but decided little crow, Mrs. Cluck was so perfectly indignant to think that a daughter of hers should turn out a crowing hen that she quite forgot to scold the cock, who really was at the bottom of all the mischief. And she threatened the little hen with such dire punishment if ever she should be heard to crow again that that no doubt would have been the last of it if it had not been for the cock. Whenever he and his sister were far enough away for their mother not to hear, he persuaded the little hen to crow, until she was known all through the chicken-yard as "the crowing hen;" and it even reached the ears of the farmer's wife, who was very much annoyed, and said solemnly, and without the slightest regard for Brown's Grammar, which she had studied in her early youth,

> "'Whistling girls and crowing hens
> Never comes to no good ends.'"

As the two grew up things became worse and worse. The cock seemed to take a perfect delight in leading the poor simple hen into all sorts of mischief, and then leaving her to take the scolding or punishment that followed. He had great faith in his own cleverness, and he made use of the little hen's admiration of him to teach her a great many wrong things, such as scratching up garden-seed, and eating the ripe tomatoes, and roosting on the front porch instead of in the chicken-house; in short, everything he could think of that he knew was forbidden. He did not imagine that the farmer's wife was watching him until one dreadfully rainy morning, when he and his sister and a few more of the chickens had taken refuge under a bench by the kitchen-door. There had been a long drought, and the great rain-water cask had begun to split with the heat, so that now, as the rain poured into it, little waterfalls came bursting out between the staves; and under one of these cascades the mischievous cock persuaded the poor silly hen to stand till she was soaked through. She did not like it at all, and squawked and danced about like a wild Indian, but he kept saying, "It'll make your feathers grow, dear, and perhaps a fine comb, like mine, on top of your head."

The farmer's wife was standing at the kitchen-door watching the rain, and when she saw the foolish hen standing under the waterfall, and heard her squawking and screaming, and saw the cock enjoying it so much that he forgot to go under the bench out of the rain, she turned to her daughter, and said, "There's that simple hen again! She doesn't even know enough to go in when it rains; and that's the cock who is always in mischief. You catch them both to-night, Sally, after they've gone to roost: we'll put them up for a couple of weeks to fatten, and have them for your father's birthday. That hen's too foolish to live, and the cock's altogether too smart."

"LITTLE WATERFALLS CAME BURSTING OUT BETWEEN THE STAVES."

See Page 170.

So, two weeks from that day the mischievous cock and the silly hen were simply a pair of roast chickens, and Mrs. Cluck said solemnly to the rest of her children, "You can't all be clever, but if you are foolish, you can follow a good example as well as you can a bad one; and if you are really clever, your cleverness will keep you out of mischief and out of disgrace."

DARING.

"BUT I don't see *why* we must give up Don, mamma," said little Annie Cameron, half pouting and half crying, as she fed Don from her hand for the last time. The sale was to take place that day: poor Don was only "Lot 90" now, instead of a petted and spoiled favorite. It was no wonder that Annie felt like crying, but it grieved her mother to see the pout.

"I thought papa explained it very fully to you last night, dear," said Mrs. Cameron gently. "You know we must choose between being separated from him all the week except Sunday, and leaving this place, which we all love, for a home in town, where he can come every night; and surely you do not love this house and Don better than you love your father?"

"You know I don't, mamma," said Annie indignantly, "but I think papa might put Don to board somewhere: you heard him say that if everything went well we might be able to have a country home again in three or four years."

"SHE FED DON FROM HER HAND FOR THE LAST TIME." See Page 174.

"He cannot afford to pay board for Don, as I think you know," replied Mrs. Cameron; "and he did his very best to find some trustworthy person who would be willing to keep Don for the sake of using him, before he offered him for sale. But you must say good-bye to him now, and come with me to the station: it is almost time for our train, and quite time for people to begin to come to the sale, and I wish to go before any one comes."

The good-bye was said with many tears and kisses. Don was a remarkably gentle and affectionate horse, and what made the parting particularly hard was the fact that Annie had just begun riding him. Before they knew that it would be necessary to leave the country home Mrs. Cameron had made Annie a pretty riding-dress, and Mr. Cameron was teaching her to ride. She had not yet gone outside their own grounds, but she was hoping soon to take a "real ride" on the road with her father, and the removal to a city home and the parting from Don were bitter trials. She did not consider that her mother was giving up quite as much in making the change as she was, and that her regrets were altogether selfish.

She was an only child, and had been ill a good deal; this had caused her to be indulged much more than she would otherwise have been, and she was rapidly growing both selfish and exacting.

The new home was a very pleasant one, situated in a large country-town which had not yet begun to call itself a city. The house was cheerful and comfortable, and there was a yard which almost amounted to a garden behind it, while a small lawn in front and at the sides removed it a little from the street and from the neighboring houses. Annie found some little pleasure in helping her mother to arrange the familiar furniture in the unfamiliar rooms, but when this was done, and her own possessions had been bestowed to the best advantage in the pleasant little room allotted her, she fretted and pined for the country home in a manner which greatly distressed her mother.

The move had been made in the early summer, and Mrs. Cameron, who dearly loved flowers, tried to interest Annie in the somewhat neglected flower-beds and shrubs about the house; but Annie declared that there was not room enough to make anything worth while, and what little help she gave her mother was given reluctantly and ungraciously, so that Mrs. Cameron was quite surprised one day when Annie came running briskly in from the yard with a flushed and cheerful face, exclaiming, "Oh, mamma, I've made a friend! Such a dear little girl lives next door! We've been talking over the wall, and she is going to ask her mother to let her come and see me this afternoon; and may I ask her to stay to tea?"

"I would rather see her first, dear," said Mrs. Cameron gently. "You know I shall be delighted for you to have a little companion if I find her a suitable one for you, but the people in this neighborhood are perfect strangers to us, and it would be awkward for you to be obliged to draw back if she should not turn out just what you think her now."

"But, indeed, mamma," said Annie positively, "she's as nice as she can be. I have been talking with her for an hour, and I kept thinking all the time how much you'd like her."

"WE'VE BEEN TALKING OVER THE WALL."

"I hope I shall," said Mrs. Cameron, "and if I do, you shall spend as much time with her as you can. Did she tell you her name?"

"She said it was Ada Hebbard," replied Annie, a little sullenly, "and that her mamma meant to call on you very soon."

"I hope she will do so," said Mrs. Cameron, "if she is the lady who lives on our right hand, and whom I have seen passing several times: she has a very pleasant face."

"Then I *may* ask Ada to tea?" said Annie eagerly.

"Dear child," said her mother, "you will be much happier, and so shall I, when you have learned 'to take no for an answer.' I must see your little friend before I allow you to become so intimate with her."

Mrs. Hebbard herself called that afternoon, bringing little Ada with her. She was gentle and refined, and Mrs. Cameron felt entirely satisfied before the visit was over that Annie had found a safe and pleasant companion. Her only fear was that Annie's rather imperious disposition would take advantage of Ada's amiability.

The little girls became almost inseparable, and Annie was quite inconsolable when she learned that Mrs. Hebbard and Ada were going to the seashore for July and August.

After they went she fretted and grieved until she was really ill, and her father, who feared that the change from her country home was injuring her, proposed to Mrs. Cameron that she should take Annie to the quiet boarding-place where Mrs. Hebbard and Ada had gone, and leave her for a week in charge of Mrs. Hebbard, who had kindly suggested the plan before she went. This was finally decided upon, and Annie was at once wildly happy. Her mother took her to Mrs. Hebbard's boarding-place, and, after

"AN OLD SAILOR WAS TALKING TO ONE OF THE SUMMER BOARDERS."

spending a pleasant day on the beach, arranged to come again in ten days with Mr. Cameron, and, after staying a week at the seashore, bring her little daughter home.

Annie's weariness and listlessness were soon forgotten. The daily bath and walk on the sunny pier, the interest of watching the arrival and departure of the great steamboat which carried excursionists to and fro, the hunts for shells and sea-weed, made the days seem only too short.

One breezy day, when she and Ada, with arms affectionately linked, were walking back and forth upon the pier, they stopped to listen to an old sailor who was talking to one of the summer boarders, who sometimes employed him to take them fishing and sailing.

"She's a brave little girl," he was saying. "When those boys capsized their boat the other day out there beyond the breakers, she never waited to scream nor call for help, nor nothing, but into her father's boat she jumped, and hoisted the sail, and was out there among them before you could say 'Jack Robinson;' and she kept her head so steady, and went to work with so much sense, that not a one of them was drowned."

"Oh, please tell me who it was," cried Annie excitedly; "I should like so much to see her!"

"It's my little daughter, miss," said the sailor, turning to Annie with a pleasant smile, "and you can see her a'most any day you choose to come down to the cove. Whenever my boat's out she runs down to the beach a dozen times to see if she can spy me coming in. Our house is down by the old pier, and she's the housekeeper: she cooks and scrubs, and washes and irons, and

"THEY FOUND HER STANDING IN THE COVE BESIDE THE OLD PIER."

See Page 185.

always has me a good supper or dinner, as the case may be, ready as soon as I come in."

"Is she all alone while you are out?" asked Ada, who had listened with deep interest.

"Yes, miss," he answered, a little sadly; "her mother died when she was a mite of a baby, and she and I have taken care of each other ever since."

"We'll come down to the old pier to-morrow," said Annie decidedly. "I want to see her and tell her how brave I think she is."

"She'll be glad enough to see you, my little ladies," said the sailor, looking very much pleased. "I often fret myself with thinking how lonesome she must be when I'm away, and, for the matter of that, when I'm there too, for I'm quiet company for a bright little thing like her. I've engaged to take a party out early tomorrow morning, and we'll likely be back about one o'clock, so if you go down to the old pier between twelve and one, you'll be pretty sure of finding my little Amy on the beach."

The children went home full of talk about their little heroine, and Mrs. Hebbard willingly agreed to walk with them to the old pier the next morning to see her. She thought that perhaps she could in some way befriend the lonely little girl, and that it would, at any rate, give her pleasure to see Annie and Ada.

They found her the next morning, as her father had said, standing in the pebbly cove beside the old pier, shading her eyes with her hand as she watched his boat come in. She was a slender but strong and healthy-looking girl of about fourteen, with a sun-browned face and bright, pleasant eyes. She seemed very glad to see the little girls, and invited them to come and rest in the vine-covered porch of the small house, which stood far enough back from the sea for grass and trees and shrubbery to grow around it, although on this part of the coast there were "green things growing" almost down to the narrow strip of beach-sand which bordered the sea.

Mrs. Hebbard declined at first, thinking that the sailor would want his dinner, and they would be in the way, but Amy, guessing her reason, said smilingly, "Indeed, ma'am, father won't be ready for his dinner this half hour: he never will leave the boat, after it has been used, until he's mopped up the deck and sponged off the paint; he's as particular with it as I am with the house."

"Then we will sit down for a few minutes," said Mrs. Hebbard, "for these little girls wish very much to hear from your own lips about your courageous act the other day."

Amy did not seem to understand for a moment, and then she laughed and blushed, saying, "It was nothing so very courageous, ma'am: I'm so used to the water that it was quite safe for me, and if I had waited to call any one it might have been too late."

Annie and Ada asked many eager questions, all of which the child answered pleasantly and readily, but it was quite evident that she did not in the least regard herself as a heroine, or even think that she had been brave.

"A LITTLE BASKET, FILLED WITH A CAT-BIRD'S NEST, SWUNG FROM A BOUGH."

See page 189

When they asked her if she were never lonely, she said, hesitatingly, "Well, not exactly lonely, for I can almost always find something to do, but I do sometimes wish that I had some lesson-books. I've read all the books on the shelf, some of them two or three times, and there are winter evenings and times like them when I could study nicely if I only had the books."

"If you will come and see us to-morrow afternoon, said Mrs. Hebbard, "we will have a talk about it, and I think I can send you enough school-books for next winter, at least, when I go home. I have a good many which Ada's older sister used, and it would give me pleasure to send them to you."

Amy thanked Mrs. Hebbard very gratefully, and promised to come. Then, as they rose to go, she led the way to a clump of bushes near the kitchen-door.

"I always have plenty of company in summer," she said, smiling. "Ever since I hung a basket here three years ago I have a family of tenants who pay me in music."

Parting the boughs, she disclosed a little basket swinging from a branch and filled with a cat-bird's nest, in which a half-fledged bird was opening its mouth to be fed, while the mother hovered anxiously about, evidently in doubt as to what these intrusive people meant to do.

"She doesn't mind me at all, she's so used to me," said Amy, "but strangers frighten her a little. There were two more, and I've been fretting a good deal, because I'm afraid the cat has got them. They were standing on the edge of the nest, trying to fly, yesterday, and I haven't seen them since."

The children were greatly interested, and would have stayed longer, but Mrs. Hebbard saw the sailor coming, and they bade Amy good-bye, telling her to be sure and come the next day.

On the way home Annie could talk of nothing but Amy's courage in rescuing the boys, but Mrs. Hebbard said gently, "I think she shows the truest courage in her unselfish, toilsome daily life. She must often be lonely and tired, but she did not utter a word of complaint about anything."

Annie was silent. She could not help thinking how differently Amy would have acted from herself could they change places, and how impatiently and fretfully she would behave under a small part of Amy's privations.

They stopped for their letters, and Ada, as she finished reading one from her father, exclaimed joyfully, "Papa says he is going to bring the new horse and your phaeton, to-morrow, mamma, and that the horse is *quite* gentle, and he is sure you can drive it."

This was welcome news. There were many pretty drives in the neighborhood, but Mrs. Hebbard had found great difficulty in hiring suitable horses, and Mr. Hebbard had been unwilling to send the new horse until he had tried it and made himself sure that it was safe. Mrs. Hebbard and the children were at the station some time before the morning-train was due the next day in their impatience to welcome Mr. Hebbard and the horse. A board was slanted from the side of the freight-car to the ground, and the horse was led carefully down, but scarcely had he reached the ground when Annie sprang forward, exclaiming, "Oh, it's Don! it's my own dear old Don!"

It was indeed, and he seemed to recognize Annie, putting down his nose to be petted and whinnying gently, as he used to do. Mr. Hebbard had bought him from a horse-dealer, so it was impossible to tell where he had been since Annie parted from him, but he had evidently been well cared for.

"Oh, if I could *only* ride him again!" said Annie impulsively as they walked back to the boarding-house.

"Why! *did* you ride him, Annie?" asked Ada in surprise.

"Yes, indeed," replied Annie; "papa was teaching me, and I used to ride nearly every day."

"How you must have hated to give him up!" said Ada, sympathizingly; and Annie assented, saying to herself, "They did not *ask* me if I rode him in the lane or on the road."

"You shall ride him again," said Mr. Hebbard kindly. "I am obliged to go back to-morrow, but Bob is a trustworthy fellow, and if he can find a horse for himself you can ride every day, if you like, after Mrs. Hebbard has taken her drive."

"Oh, thank you very much," said Annie delightedly.—"I will buy some black stuff this afternoon, Ada, and make a skirt: that black cashmere waist will do quite well."

Mrs. Hebbard had always found Annie truthful, and it never

occurred to any of them to question her statement that she had often ridden Don. Amy came that afternoon while they were busy over the skirt, and insisted upon helping, so that by evening it was quite done, and Annie promised to go to the old pier for her very first ride and let Amy see how well it looked. Mr. Hebbard had advised her to wait a few days, until Don should be quite over the nervousness of the journey; and she was very willing to do this, for, while she was not a little elated with the prospect of a " real " ride, with a groom in attendance, she quaked a little at the thought of riding Don without her father at hand to direct and encourage her. No one would have suspected this, however, from her smiling face when the afternoon at last came and Don was led to the door. She set off gayly, waving her hand to Mrs. Hebbard and Ada, who watched her from the piazza. But she soon found that it required a strong hand and fixed attention to manage the spirited horse, who had been well fed and lightly worked, and she would have given much before the end of the straggling village-street was reached to be safely out of the enterprise. Nothing but a very false pride restrained her from returning even then and owning the truth. She was trying to convince herself that it would be foolish to do this when a dog suddenly sprang toward the horse, barking loudly. Don shied violently, almost throwing her from the saddle, and then broke into a run, paying no attention whatever to her frantic tugs at the bridle. The noise made by the groom and the blacksmith and the dog in pursuit, and the screaming of one or

"A BOY BY THE WAYSIDE BRAVELY SEIZED THE BRIDLE, AND HELD HIM."

See Page 195.

two thoughtless women, increased Don's fright; he looked behind him, as horses so often do when running away, and Annie would no doubt have been dashed from the saddle in another moment, when a boy who was digging sods by the roadside, seeing the horse coming, bravely stood in his path and seized the bridle. He managed to hold on until the groom and the blacksmith came up, and then, with a cry of pain, he let go his hold; his shoulder had been put out of joint by the last desperate pull which Don had given to the reins. Annie was quite unhurt, but weak and trembling with fright, and her confession, first to Mrs. Hebbard, and a few days later to her mother, was a very humble one.

"I thought I was being very brave, mamma, when I mounted Don," she said, "but I see now that I was a coward; I was afraid to own that I had told what was not true about riding Don; for it was just the same as an untruth, although the words themselves were true, and so I came near being killed myself, and have been the cause of all the pain that poor brave boy is suffering."

"It is much harder to have the kind of courage in which you were wanting, my poor little girl," said her mother, "than it is to have mere physical courage, which often amounts to nothing but foolhardiness. You have had a serious lesson, and I hope it will teach you that there is a higher and better pleasure than that of having one's own way."

Annie proved the sincerity of her repentance by asking that a promised birthday-party might be given up, and that she might take the money which it would have cost, together with a gold-piece which she had been treasuring for the purchase of a paint-box, to the brave little fellow who had risked his life to save hers. This was done, and although he at first refused to take it, Mrs. Cameron finally succeeded in convincing him that it was not right to let the expense of the accident fall upon his mother, who could ill afford it. And Annie showed her gratitude while they remained in the neighborhood by daily visits and many little acts of kindness.

THE END OF THE RAINBOW.

IT was evening, and the children,
    Who had been away to glean,
Were laughing and dancing and shouting
    Upon the village-green;
For Jan, their prince and leader—
    A fearless lad and bold—
Showed them a whole month's wages,
    A shining piece of gold.

She's a funny little body,
  That little Mat of ours;
If we take her out a-gleaning,
  She stops to gather flowers.
When she saw the shining gold-piece
  In Jan's hand, little Mat
Said, " Where shall I find them growing,
  Such flowers, Jan, as that?"

Jan laughed with his hearty laughter,
  And said to little Mat,
" The next time there's a rainbow,
  You go to the end of that,
And there'll you'll find gold-pieces,
  And diamonds and pearls,
Enough for yourself, my beauty,
  And all the little girls."

And to think that she believed him!
  She never once let on,
But last night there came a rainbow,
  And little Mat was gone.
It was just as the sun was setting:
  We were rushing back to play
On the green, for the shower was over
  That had scattered us away.

She went through
  the briery pas-
  ture,
Where the bars
  had been let
  down,
For we found upon
  the briers
  Scraps of her little
  gown;
And then there came
  a wheatfield,
  And such tiny, tiny
  feet
As our Mat's would
  leave no track
  there
  In passing through
  the wheat.

"SHE WENT THROUGH THE BRIERY PASTURE."

So we searched and called and wandered
  For an hour, father and I;
And at last I was so frightened
  That I could not help but cry;

For, you see, she is so little,
　　And it was nearly dark,
But before I was fairly crying
　　I heard the puppy bark.

"SHE WAS LYING THERE, THE DARLING!"

I hadn't thought of the puppy—
　　He follows her all about—

And as soon as we heard him barking,
   At once we spied her out.
She was lying there, the darling!
   By his side, asleep in peace,
And he was bravely barking
   At a flock of prying geese.

Father picked her up in a minute—
   We hadn't the heart to scold—
And she said to me, "Oh, sister,
   I did not find the gold.
I saw the end of the rainbow
   In this wheatfield from our gate,
But it was gone when I got here:
   I suppose I was too late."

A COUNTRY MONTH.

MR. and Mrs. Holman, and Cecil and Agnes, were sitting at breakfast in a cheerful, pleasant breakfast-room. The postman had just rung the bell and left several letters, and Mrs. Holman was reading one. It must have had something pleasant in it, for she smiled several times as she read it, until the children, both at once, burst out, "What is it, mamma? Read it aloud, please."

But she kept quietly on to the end, as if she had not heard them, and when she had finished she turned to their father, saying quite gravely, though a smile lurked in her eyes and in the corners of her mouth, "Don't you think, papa, that Agnes and Cecil are looking a little pale and thin?"

Mr. Holman looked at his children anxiously, but not even the most anxious parent could have seen anything but health and

"THAT LOVELY BATH IN THE WATER-BUTT WAS TOO COLD FOR HER."

See Page 206.

strength in the two rosy faces which shone above two large bowls of porridge and milk. "Why no, dear," he said, "I can't say that I do ; what put such an idea into your head?"

"Well," said Mrs. Holman, twisting the letter in her fingers, "it occurred to me that they had both done very well at school this last term, and that they needed a little change of air and scene."

"Oh, I know what it is," exclaimed Agnes joyfully: "we're invited to Aunt and Uncle Pennell's ; they said we must come in the holidays.—You'll let us go, mamma ; you *will*, won't you?"

"It's a clear case of mind-reading," said Mr. Holman, as he saw by his wife's smile that Agnes had guessed right. "You'll have to stop thinking when these children are about, mamma."

Aunt and Uncle Pennell lived on a large farm in a wild, beautiful part of Pennsylvania, and they contended that the scenery by which they were surrounded quite made up to them for the hilliness and stoniness of their farm. They had no children, and the delight was always mutual when Agnes and Cecil visited them.

A joyful note of preparation sounded through the house. Uncle Pennell had written that he would have business in town the next day but one after his letter reached them, and that he hoped the children would be ready to return with him. So, while Mrs. Holman packed such trifling matters as clothes and shoes, Cecil and Agnes attended to fishing-lines and landing-nets and their new croquet set and a large family of dolls—so large that all could not go, and a heartrending choice must be made—half to go and half to stay.

"I suppose you'll take that gorgeous thing you got last Christmas?" said Cecil, who tolerated dolls, and even made furniture, because, as he said, "Agnes is jolly good company in all the games I like; so of course I'm civil to her dolls, though I can't see much sense in them."

"No," said Agnes, thoughtfully. "Lady Geraldine is looking very well; and besides, I don't believe the sun would be good for her complexion: we shall be out of doors most of the time, you know. I am picking out the ones who haven't been well. There is poor Clarissa, who has never seemed quite the same since I gave her that lovely bath in the water-butt; it was too cold for her, I'm afraid. She's the worst of all, but there are five more who haven't looked well lately, so I shall take those six."

"You wouldn't look well yourself," said Cecil, "if somebody'd knocked your nose off, or let half the stuffing out of you, or pulled all your hair off, or sewed your arms on hind-part before, or lost one of your legs."

"I have hopes of all of them except poor Berengaria," said Agnes sadly: "I don't see how anything can be done for her nose. But perhaps Aunt Lucy will; she's a wonderful person to think of things. Perhaps it is because she has such nice quiet times to think in."

"She will not have them much longer," said Cecil, laughing, "but then I don't think she minds a good noise any more than mamma does."

The journey to the Hill Farm was a long and somewhat tedious

"THE COWS STOOD KNEE-DEEP IN THE LITTLE RIVER."

one, but it did not seem so to the eager children, who had been shut up in a city for nearly a year, and to whom everything they saw and heard was delightful. The large "express-wagon," with all the curtains rolled up, was waiting for them at the station, and they drove through the fields in the soft twilight, the narrow road winding away up a long hill upon the side of which the large old-fashioned house was built. The cows had been milked and turned out to pasture again, and were standing about, some on the soft grass, and some knee-deep in the little river which ran through the pasture-land. A few late bird-notes came from the woods, and everything was so lovely that they would have been sorry that the drive should come to an end if it had not been for Aunt Lucy's kind welcoming face in the doorway.

They found they were more tired than they imagined, and after the good country supper was disposed of they were very glad to go to the little white-bed, smelling of lavender, which Aunt Lucy's loving hands had made ready for them; but they begged that they might be called "the first thing" in the morning, there was so much to see and to do. Their uncle had told them that the wheat-harvest was to begin the next day, and both of them expected to be very busy—Agnes with helping Aunt Lucy in her preparations for the grand harvest-home supper which always was held in the great barn as soon as the harvesting was done.

But the men with their wheat-cradles and the women who followed them to bind the sheaves had been in the wheatfield for an hour or two the next morning before the tired children woke. Aunt Lucy had gone to call them, but they were sleeping so soundly that, as she said to Uncle John, she "hadn't the heart to wake them till they'd had their sleep out;" so she saved them some breakfast, and laughed at their reproaches when they came down, toward eight o'clock, thoroughly rested and ready for anything.

There was only one drawback to Agnes's enjoyment when she stayed at Hill Farm: she was terribly afraid of cows. In vain Cecil, who was not afraid of anything, fed and caressed the pretty, gentle creatures at milking-time; Agnes always preferred to be on the other side of the fence while this operation was being performed.

"CECIL FED THE COWS OUT OF HIS HAND."

"I know all about it, Cecil," she would say. "They look as gentle as dear little lambs while they are eating things out of your hand in that way, and while Nanny is milking them, but nobody can tell what they are thinking about: they may be intending to spear you with their horns the very next minute; and when they have you between them and the fence they make most dreadful faces at you with their great eyes."

And nothing that Cecil could say gave Agnes any confidence in cows.

While they were still lingering over their saved breakfast, discussing the cow question, Uncle John came in from the harvest-field warm and thirsty, and very glad to find Aunt Lucy's bright pail of raspberry vinegar, with a lump of ice floating in it and a new tin dipper tied to the pail, waiting in the back porch to be carried to the field.

"That's good!" he said as he emptied the dipper. "I never found a drink yet, Lucy, that I liked better than this of a hot day. I wonder if there's a smart boy of nine or ten anywhere around here who'd like a job for the morning?" he added, turning with a smile to the children.

"Here's one, sir, all ready for anything," said Cecil, jumping up.

"Well, then, ask Aunt Lucy for a basket, and come with me to the orchard," said Uncle John. "There's a tree full of harvest apples there spoiling to be picked, and the men would think I was crazy if I took one of them from the wheat-cutting such weather as this. We'll pick them on shares: you keep count of your baskets, and I'll send you down half what you've picked in winter apples this fall, for these will have to go to market right off. They don't keep long, but they sell like hot cakes. How will that suit you?"

"Splendidly!" said Cecil, joyfully.—" Just think, Agnes, of having ever so many apples all our own, in the fall! We can take some to everybody at school for days and days."

So Cecil went joyfully with his uncle to the orchard, and spent a busy morning among the harvest apples, while Agnes followed Aunt Lucy from the great airy kitchen, with its painted floor and raftered ceiling, to the delightfully cool dairy and cellars, helping with whatever willing little hands could do, and looking on admiringly when she could not help.

But Aunt Lucy did not mean her little girl to spend the whole of that bright day in the house; so after dinner, when a light breeze sprang up and some white clouds came skimming across the sun, she said to her, "You've done all you can now, little maid, and I want you to put on your hat and go down the lane to the spring-house—it's shady nearly all the way—and where the spring comes out from the rocks, just above the house, you'll find such a tangle of ferns and wild roses and honeysuckle as you haven't seen since the last time you were here; and I want enough to fill the big brown pitcher. Your uncle loves to see flowers on the tea-table, and I always pick them for him when I have time, but I thought perhaps you'd take that much of the housekeeping off my hands while you're here."

"Oh, aunty, that will be delightful!" said Agnes eagerly, "there are such heaps of flowers about here! I'll go right away, and do you want me to hurry back?"

"No, dear; stay as long as you please, and go on to the orchard and harvest-field if you like," replied Aunt Lucy, smiling. "You'll hear the horn at half-past five, and that will be time enough for you to come back. You can arrange them while you're out there, and then it'll not take a minute to put them in the pitcher."

It was a very happy little girl who went wandering down the green, shady lane which led to the spring-house, singing little snatches of song and thinking what a letter full of things she already had to write to her mother. And her happiness rose to rapture when she found the tangle of sweet things of which her aunt had told her. She sat with her hands clasped, feeling as if it would be too bad to spoil the beauty of the little nook by picking anything; and she had nearly fallen asleep in the sweet, warm, drowsy air when somebody suddenly said, "Boo!" close by her ear, and she sprang up, startled, to see her uncle's laughing face peeping at her through an opening in the honeysuckle vines.

"SHE WAS STARTLED AT SEEING HER UNCLE'S FACE."

"And what are you doing here, I should like to know," said Uncle John, "falling asleep among the leaves, like a babe in the woods?"

"I came to pick some flowers for aunty, Uncle John," answered Agnes, quite awake now and making a vigorous attack upon the honeysuckle; "but everything looked so lovely that it almost seemed as if I oughtn't to, and I didn't know I was asleep at all till you 'boo'd' at me. You oughtn't to do such things, dear: don't you know that when people are very badly frightened their hair sometimes turns perfectly white right away?"

"I never thought of that," said Uncle John gravely, "but I'll try and remember it the next time. You leave your posies here in the spring, Pussy, and come with me to the harvest-field. I've something to show you, and I was coming to the house to call you when I spied you here. We'll call Cecil as we go by the orchard; he's dreadfully busy, but perhaps he can spare himself for five minutes."

So Agnes put her bunch of honeysuckle carefully in a little basin on one side of the stream, and skipped along by Uncle John's side, helping him give a loud "halloo" to Cecil as they passed the orchard. They found quite an excitement when they came to the harvest-field. The woman who lived in the tenant-house was there, with her baby in her arms and another clinging to her skirts, and several of the laborers' children were there too; and the oldest reaper pointed the children to a beautiful little nest on the ground, right in the midst of the great wheatfield, with three white eggs in it. Cecil came running up, and he and Agnes bent over the nest, thinking it the prettiest thing they had ever seen.

"But where is the mother-bird?" asked Agnes. "She ought to be here taking care of her eggs."

"She was scared away hours ago, my dear," said the man. "It's a lark's nest; they always build on the ground, poor foolish things!

"ONE OF THE MEN POINTED TO A NEST ON THE GROUND."

and I doubt if she ever comes back: they're easily frightened off. It won't do to leave the nest here—it would be sure to be tramped on—but you might take it up carefully and put it in the fence-corner, and if she's coming back she'll find it after we've gone this evening and everything's quiet."

So Agnes and Cecil carefully lifted the pretty nest and put it safely in the fence-corner, but the mother-lark never came back to it: she had been too badly frightened; so, after waiting two or three days to make sure, the children brought the nest to the house and Uncle John showed them how to "blow" the eggs. The nest would be a great ornament for their cabinet next winter.

It was not until Agnes was in bed that evening, and just falling into a delightful sleep, that she remembered her unfortunate children, brought to the country for their health and then left for a whole night and day packed in a dismal trunk. But sleep was too strong for her; she only had time to murmur to herself, "I'll beg all their pardons to-morrow," and then she knew nothing more till morning.

And lo and behold! when she waked with the sunshine streaming into her room, and feeling as if she had been roused by somebody's laughing, there sat the whole six, in chairs adapted to their various sizes, by her bed, and she pinched herself to see if she were dreaming. Then she saw that Berengaria was proudly holding aloft a perfectly-restored nose, and was once more the elegant and gracious lady who had come to delight Agnes's heart the previous Christmas; and she saw that the chairs were ingeniously made of slender cornstalks, bound together with packthread, and that in the lap of the black Dinah, who had been brought on account of her missing leg, lay a very funny cornhusk baby.

Agnes felt as if she could scarcely wait to wash and dress, she was in such a hurry to get down stairs and solve the mystery. It

"SHE FOUND THE TENANT'S DAUGHTER ON HER KNEES BEFORE BERENGARIA."

was easily solved. Aunt Lucy had found the neglected children when she unpacked Agnes's trunk and put her clothes in bureau and closet, and she had mended Berengaria's nose with some wax left from making wax flowers, and put a delicate coat of paint on it, the evening before after Agnes was in bed, while Uncle John made the cornstalk chairs and the cornhusk baby.

"I think I'll take Berengaria out in the little grove and seat her under a pine tree as long as the weather is good, aunty," said Agnes after breakfast. "I've heard mamma say there's nothing so restoring as pine-air."

So the invalid was dressed in her walking-suit and new summer hat, and seated on a soft cushion of moss against a fallen pine tree to recover her strength, while her thoughtful mother went to the raspberry-patch to help Aunt Lucy pick raspberries. both,. for tea that evening and for jam to-morrow.

And when Agnes went, just before dinner, to bring her child home, she found the tenant's little daughter—whom she had seen in the hayfield the day before—on her knees before the beautiful stranger in rapt admiration. She was holding by the arm a doll made out of a round white radish, of great size for a radish: this was the head; the body and arms were merely two sticks lashed together at right angles; and this very primitive doll had on for her sole garment an equally primitive calico frock, which had a good deal more pinning and tying than sewing about it.

Little Sally's admiration for the city lady was so sincere, and at the same time so free of envy or of dislike to her own home-made doll, that Agnes resolved, if Aunt Lucy would help her—and of course she would—to make and dress a good large "rag doll," neatly shaped and with a face painted, instead of cut in gashes.

This was successfully done before Agnes went home, and her happiest recollection of that overflowingly happy visit was the beaming face of little Sally as she clasped her new treasure to her heart and promised to "be the very best mother in all the world to her, and to name her Agnes."

Aunt Lucy had known Sally ever since she was a baby; she knew her to be a gentle and well-behaved little girl, and so she was very glad for Agnes to have some one so

near her own age for a playmate. Hand in hand the two little girls wandered about the place when Agnes was not busy "helping"—from the old-fashioned kitchen-garden, where wall-fruit and vegetables and beds of sweet herbs grew, through the arch to the large front yard, where nothing was permitted to grow but grass and trees and ornamental shrubs, with one large bed of bright flowers in the middle of the lawn. Agnes rather pitied Cecil because he had not found a friend too, but he told her she needn't be uneasy—that everybody was his friend, from Aunt Lucy down to Jet, the beautiful black setter. Jet was a rather reserved dog, devoted to his master and mistress, and to Joe, the faithful "headman," who stayed at the farm the year round.

"You and little Miss Agnes ought to feel very proud that Jet's taken to you so, Master Cecil," said Joe gravely. He was taking his "noon-spell" on a shady bank, with Jet at his feet, and, having finished his dinner, was whittling out for Cecil one of the willow whistles for which he was justly famous.

"Jet's a little like me," continued Joe; "he don't take up with everybody that comes along before he sees what they're like; but once let him settle in his mind that he'll be friends with any one, and he *is* friends for all time;" and Joe tested his whistle with a long, shrill blast that made Jet start to his feet in astonishment.

The harvesting was finished, and the long table, made of trestles and boards, was spread in the orchard for the harvest-home supper. And what a merry supper it was! Aunt Lucy's gentle face at the

"JOE WAS WHITTING OUT A WILLOW WHISTLE FOR CECIL."   See Page 226.

head of the table kept the merriment within pleasant bounds ; and Uncle John told stories ; and Joe, after a great deal of persuasion, sang a song; and Cecil, by special request, recited "Marco Bozzaris" with appropriate gestures, that being his last declamation before he left school. The great moon was rising behind the trees before the company rose from the table, and they had hardly separated before Joe came to the front porch—where Aunt Lucy and Uncle John and 'the children had seated themselves to enjoy the moonlight for a while before going to bed—in a great state of excitement, to say that a herd of deer was coming down the hill to the pond in the newly-cleared ground just above the house, and that if the children would come with him very softly along the edge of the wood, they might perhaps get a sight of them, as the wind was blowing toward the wood, and so the deer would not scent them. The children had often heard that there were deer in the tract of wild land on top of the hill, but they had never had the good luck to see them, and they sprang up in great delight and followed Joe to the edge of the wood, stealing along in the moonlight like conspirators bent on mischief. They hid themselves behind a clump of bushes, through which they could peep, and had only waited a few minutes when the herd went softly stepping past. Two beautiful fawns, a little more than half grown, came first, then the doe, and last, like the rear-guard of an army, a stag with magnificent branching antlers. Although Joe and the children stood perfectly still, almost holding their breath as the deer passed, the pretty creatures seemed to have an instinctive feeling that their solitude was invaded. They turned their heads toward the thicket,

"TWO FAWNS, THEN THE DOE, AND THEN THE STAG."

sniffing the air with a distrustful, startled expression, but they did not run; and when they had passed out of sight Agnes said softly, "Let us go home very quietly, or they'll be scared away before they have had their drink."

The children never forgot the beautiful moonlit picture which the deer had made.

"I have ever so many lovely things hung up in my head to keep looking at after I go home, Aunt Lucy," said Agnes the next day when she was describing the herd of deer to her aunt and trying to make her understand that the moonlight made them look like "fairy deer."

After the harvest was over there was time for a day's fishing,

"AN OLD MILL WHICH WAS FAST TURNING INTO A PICTURESQUE RUIN."

which had been postponed because "it would keep" and the fun and festivities of harvest would not. It was to be a picnic as well as a fishing-excursion, and Aunt Lucy and Uncle John had promised to give up a whole day to it. Beef was roasted, and eggs were boiled, and cake was made, the day before, and Joe brought in a great basketful of raspberries while they were at breakfast.

Four or five miles higher up the hill—which, if it had stood alone instead of in a chain, would have been called a very respectable mountain—was an old mill which had not been running for several years, and which was fast turning into a very picturesque ruin. It had been stopped by a singular accident, and one at which the miller had grumbled more than a little. A tunnel had been cut through the hill, and, as the miller said, had "knocked the bottom out of the springs" which had fed his mill-stream. There was still a tiny stream, except in very dry weather, and a pretty pond was left, having been, fortunately, in a sort of natural basin a little to one side of the tunnel. Behind the mill was a grove of beautiful oak and hickory trees, with short, velvety grass growing underneath them; and it was here that Aunt Lucy settled herself with a new book and her knitting while Uncle John went with the children to the deepest side of the pond and helped them fish. They caught enough perch and sunfish to make a tempting hot dish to add to the cold dinner, and Uncle John showed them how to wrap the fish in leaves and roast them in hot ashes. It was a long, happy day, and to the little city children the perfect stillness and remoteness of the place formed its chief beauty. Sitting in the grove and looking down the hill, not a single house was in sight, and, as Cecil said, it seemed as if they were "thousands of miles away from everywhere." They had brought little Sally with them, and after dinner was over and the baskets repacked they wandered through the old mill, playing "Hide and Seek," and "Follow my Leader." Uncle John made the best "leader;" he did nothing which the children found it impossible to follow, but he went from one thing to another with such quickness and agility that the chil-

"A FROG HAD FALLEN INTO THE CLUTCHES OF A WHITE GOOSE."

dren had brisk work to follow him. When they were quite tired out they rested on the bank, watching a flock of geese and ducks that were paddling in the pond. An unwary frog had fallen into the clutches of the largest white goose, and the rest of the flock had determined to share the prize. The white goose was equally determined to keep it for herself, and she very nearly choked as she paddled off, swallowing the poor frog with all her might while she tried to keep ahead of the others.

"If it was anybody but a goose," said Agnes indignantly, "she'd be ashamed to be so selfish and greedy."

Uncle John laughed a little. "That's a good thing to remember," he said.

They stayed till dusk, eating supper while it was still broad daylight, and winding slowly down the hill just as the sun had set and while the sky was still beautiful with the "after-glow." The moon rose just before they reached home. Aunt Lucy had been persuaded to sing, the rest joined in whenever they knew the tunes, and Joe told them, as he helped them out of the wagon, that it was "as good as a concert." To the children it was better than the best concert they had ever heard.

The happy days flew by, full of different plans and occupations. Mr. and Mrs. Holman were coming for the last half of the month, and after they arrived there were daily walks and drives, and more picnics, and another fishing-party to a "real" trout-stream on one of the other hills, where the streams had not had "the bottom knocked out of them."

It was hard work to leave the lovely Hill Farm, even with the hope of returning next year and of the winter visit from Uncle John and Aunt Lucy in the interval. Mr. Holman was so touched by the sorrow of his children at being obliged to return to the crowded city that he promised solemnly that the minute he owned a million dollars he would buy a whole mountain as near the Hill Farm as he could find one for sale, build a palatial mansion on it, take lessons in farming, and move everything and everybody belonging to him up there "for good."

"Ah, papa," said Agnes mournfully when this brilliant plan had been fully discussed, "do you know what Joe used to say when we believed 'as many as six impossible things before breakfast'? He used to say, '*When* the sky falls we shall catch larks;' and I'm afraid this beautiful fairy lark won't be caught *till* the sky falls."

OLD NURSE.

O H, there's plenty of fun in summer,
    As long as the long days last,
And when they are at the longest
    They only go too fast.
We wade in the brook together,
    We scatter the new-mown hay,
And yet we are never sorry
    When there comes a rainy day.

The clouds bring rain to the flowers,
    But they do not bring us gloom,
For we run between the showers,
    To old Nurse's house and room.
She sits there all day spinning,
    But her wheel forgets to whirl
As she tells us tales beginning,
    "When I was a little girl."

Sometimes she tells of the " good folk,"
    Who, ever so long ago,

Were alive in her dear old Ireland,
    And helped good people so;
And sometimes of the famine;
    And no matter how hard we try

"SOMETIMES SHE TELLS OF THE 'GOOD FOLKS.'"

To help it, the things she tell us
    Of the famine make us cry.

To think of the little babies,
    So innocent and sweet,

Dying slowly, only just because
    There was not enough to eat!
I do *not* like rice-pudding,
    But I've eaten it since she told
Of those hapless people in Ireland
    Pinched with hunger and cold.

When our wading makes us hungry—
    We are not hard to make—
We run to Nurse, and beg her
    For some of her oatmeal cake:
That always seems to please her,
    And she gives us, too, "a sup,"
As she says, of buttermilk with it,
    In a queer old earthen cup.

So we're never tired of watching
    Her wheel as she makes it whirl,
Nor of the tales beginning,
    "When I was a little girl."
And we love to hear her tell us,
    "When I see my lassies thrive
And grow so bright and winsome,
    It keeps my heart alive."

FATHER CHRISTMAS.

WHEN grandpa came to live with us we were all very glad, for we had never had enough of him when he only came for visits or when we went to visit him; and we all of us, down to the baby, who doesn't at all like to be called "the baby," and says her name is Paulina, helped to make his room look pretty. Ailie and the little boys and Bertha and May and I brought some of our treasures to put on the wall-cabinet, and Paulina—whom we call Polly when we don't call her "the baby"—brought an old wreath of green leaves out of mamma's done-with bonnet. Polly had been wearing it all day, and was very proud of it, and she said she was going to "div it to dranpa" because it was the best thing she had. So mamma would not let us laugh at her, and put the wreath on the bureau, where grandpa would be sure to see it. He came in the morning, while we were in the school-room saying our lessons to Ailie. She has school for us every day, and mamma says that as long as we behave for her and really learn our lessons we need not go to a real school, though Ailie says that is not a compliment to her, and that if six scholars and a teacher don't make a school, she'd like to know what does. It was a very cold day the day grandpa came, and mamma and Ailie had been busy up to the day before making him a beautiful new wrapper of some thick, soft, warm stuff all trimmed with fur. When school was out we all rushed to the library to see if grandpa was there, and before we could draw the curtains he must have heard us, for he pushed them open and stood there laughing, with his new wrapper on and Polly's wreath on his head. How we all laughed and shouted, and how he hugged and kissed us!

All of a sudden Ailie said, "Grandpa, what a magnificent Kriss-Kringle you'd make, just as you are! Your name ought to be 'Father Christmas,' instead of Grandfather Hamilton."

So then we all shouted, "Father Christmas! Father Christmas!" until mamma came to see what was the matter, and said that if we made such a dreadful noise grandpa would go straight away again.

But he only laughed and said, "Not while it's a good-humored noise, Polly my dear." For he calls mamma "Polly," and it always sounds so funny to us—as if mamma were only a little girl!

When we were quiet again, grandpa said, "If I am Father Christmas, I think I have a right to say a little about my festival, but I will not say it now. I will only tell all these people who have given me my new name that they may have to pay for it before Christmas comes."

"GRANDPA STOOD THERE... WITH POLLY'S WREATH ON HIS HEAD."

See Page 234.

We were not very much afraid, and we told him so, but he laughed and shook his head at us, and told us just to wait.

Two or three days afterward, when we came to tea, we each found a note on our plate, and on it was printed, after our names, "To be opened when you are quite alone."

We could scarcely eat our suppers, we were in such a hurry to read the notes and to see what it was that made them so heavy.

I can't tell you what was in the others, except by guessing, but this was in mine: "Will my little Lou try, between this and Christmas, to overcome, with the dear Lord's help, the temper which gives mamma and herself so much pain? That will be a most joyful present for mamma. For others spend thoughtfully what you find herein, and make it give as much pleasure as it can."

And out of the envelope, as I opened it, had fallen a brand-new, shiny five-dollar gold-piece.

I cried a little at first. I knew I had a bad temper, but, somehow, I always made myself believe that anybody would have got angry about the things that made me "fly out," and I felt dreadfully ashamed to think that grandpa should have found out about me so soon; and then I began to think: "If I am ashamed for grandpa to know it, how can I bear to remember that the dear Lord knows it all the time?" I began to try that very day harder than I had ever tried before to overcome my temper; and although it often seems to me that I grow worse, instead of better, mamma says that that is because I watch myself so much more closely now than I ever did before. She always has something encouraging to say. I thought I had better tell her about my money; and I think the rest must have done it too, from what I saw afterward. You see, I could not make up my mind whether I had better count my people and divide it equally, and buy each one a little present out and out, or whether I had better buy worsteds and silks and things and make such of my presents as I could: there was still plenty of time before Christmas. So mamma said that if I could think of nice things to make my money would go a great deal further, and she thought of several things, and went with me to buy the materials; so that, with what I bought and what I made, I had ten presents to give away that Christmas—more than I had ever had before.

Fred can cut out animals and birds and dolls very nicely, and I soon found that he had plenty of nice thick bristol-board and some new paints; and in the evening, after Bertha and May, Polly and Will, had gone to bed, mamma let him stay up half an hour longer, and he made all the animals for two Noah's arks and beautiful dolls for Bertha and May and Polly. I don't know how or when he managed it, but he made something for nearly all of us—he can draw and paint and cut out so nicely—and that left him enough money to get a beautiful present for mamma. We never had such a nice Christmas before. It would take too long to tell about the different things we made, but I must tell how we begged grandpa on Christmas Day to put on his fur-trimmed wrapper, and we crowned him with a wreath of laurel and holly-berries—holly would have been prettier, but we were afraid it would stick his head—and

"FRED CAN CUT OUT ANIMALS VERY NICELY"

he sat at the head of the table in the great chair which mamma and papa had given him, with a beautiful "tidy" on its back which one of us had made, and a beautiful footstool which another of us had worked.

It was a lovely Christmas altogether. I am afraid that before that Christmas we had always thought more of what people would give us than what we should give them, and now we had been so busy planning and making things that when our presents came they were almost like a surprise.

And the only thing that any of us could possibly think of to be sorry about was that grandpa had not been with us always; but he would not let us say that; he said he would give us instead his favorite quotation: ' Look not mournfully into the past; it comes not back again: wisely improve the present; it is thine. Go forth to meet the shadowy future without fear and with a manly heart."

THE BABES IN THE WOOD.

MR. BUNNY and his wife and their family of eight children were most comfortably lodged and boarded. They had a large, pleasant hutch, with a house for rainy weather and plenty of burrowing-ground for clear days. Their little master never neglected or forgot them; there was always plenty of food, both green and dry, in the trough and in the rack, and the earthen pan was filled twice a day with clean water. When they had first come to live in the hutch, before any of their children were born, they had been frightened and uneasy, and had tried to scratch a hole and make their way out; but they found, on whichever side they began to dig, unpleasant coal-ashes and hard wooden stakes, whereas when they dug in the middle of the hutch there was only nice soft earth; so, as they found that they were well fed and cared for, they soon contented themselves with making burrows where the earth was soft, and before long had a fine range of cellars under the whole length of the hutch. And as soon as their children were old enough to listen to advice—which with rabbits is very soon—Mr. and Mrs. Bunny told them all about it, and advised them not to waste their energies in trying to dig through coal-ashes and sticks, but rather to go on improving the cellars, in which there was always plenty of work for willing paws. Sometimes an important passage-way would cave in, or they would find that a little extra digging would make a short cut, or they would decide that the underground dining-room was not large enough, and then all the paws would fall to work. But two of the eight children unfortunately heard a little girl who was watching them say to their owner, "If *I* was a rabbit, I'd never stay in a little place like this; I'd scratch out."

"But suppose you had to scratch through coal-ashes and sticks?" said the boy, laughing.

"I'd not mind the coal-ashes," persisted the little girl, "and I'd hunt round till I found a place between the sticks: there *must* be places."

Snip and Snap, who were the only ones above ground, looked at one another: here was a brand-new idea! They whispered together a good deal that day, and when night came and the rest of the family were asleep, they began to dig on the side where the earth felt softest. They soon came to the ashes; the hard bits of coal hurt their poor little paws dreadfully, but they encouraged each other, taking turns with the digging, and when they struck a

"AS THE SPARROW WENT PEEPING ABOUT HE MET A HORNED BEETLE."

See Page 245.

stake they went so carefully just on one side of it that they managed to make a narrow passage, barely large enough for one at a time to squeeze through. But their hard task had taken longer than they thought, and as first Snip, and then Snap, came wearily out of the hole into the yard, it was broad daylight, and they heard footsteps coming down the gravel-walk. They scuttled under a thick evergreen, and were barely hidden when the boy came up to the hutch.

"Hallo!" he said; "here's a bad business! I did think I'd fixed them so that they couldn't scratch out this time."

And, being a wise boy, he first repaired the breach, so that the other rabbits might not escape, and then went to look for the two missing ones, who by this time had stolen along under the hedge, and were safely—as they thought—out in the fields.

Meanwhile, poor Mr. and Mrs. Bunny were nearly distracted with alarm and anxiety. They could not go themselves in search of their disobedient children, but they begged a sparrow, who had frequently and by invitation shared their meals, to fly about the neighborhood and see if he could discover the wanderers, and tell them that if they would come home all would be forgiven.

The sparrow obligingly undertook the search, and as he went peeping about under bushes and leaves he met a large horned beetle. The beetle, who had reasons for distrusting birds, was at first not inclined to be sociable, but a few pleasant remarks from the sparrow—who had no desire to eat anything so hard and horny as the beetle—soon reassured him, and he agreed to report to the sparrow if he should see anything of the truant rabbits.

Poor little Snip and Snap were already repenting their rash act.

"What a very large place out-of-doors is!" whispered Snip as they cautiously crept along under a fence in the field adjoining the garden.

"It's a great deal too large," replied Snap piteously. "Suppose anything were to chase us, where could we hide? There'd be no time to dig a burrow, and— Oh, my goodness! what's that?"

It was only two nice little girls sitting in the middle of the field trying each other under the chin with buttercups to see if they loved butter, and laughing when they found that they both did. But rabbits with guilty consciences are easily frightened, and Snip and Snap fled for their lives. When they at last stopped running it seemed to them that they must have gone miles, and they did not in the least know where they were. They were tired out and hungry and thirsty, but they were afraid to eat any of the green things around them, because they did not look in the least like the food which the boy had brought them every day. They crouched under a hedge until it began to grow dark, and then stole timidly out into the field and nibbled at several plants, afraid to eat much of any of them. They were faint with fatigue and hunger, and presently Snip said, "I do believe that last leaf I tried was poisonous; I feel very queer indeed."

"THERE THE SPARROW FOUND THEM NEXT MORNING, ASLEEP."

See Page 249

"Oh, please don't die, Snip," wailed poor little Snap; "perhaps we can find our way back to-morrow, but I never could find it by myself."

"Well, I'll try not to die," said Snip, drowsily; and he put his paw around Snap's neck. They both fell asleep, for they were quite worn out, and there the sparrow found them the next morning; the beetle had stumbled on them in the night, and had gone to tell the sparrow as soon as it was light. They lay so still and looked so forlorn that the sparrow thought at first they were dead, but he soon saw that they were breathing, and he waited patiently till they woke. He had meant to tell them just what he thought of them on the way home, but, as he said afterward, he "hadn't the heart to." They were so broken-hearted, and so thankful to him for taking them home, that he did not scold them at all. And when the boy came out to give the Bunny family its breakfast, there were the two truants meekly waiting outside the hutch, and only too happy when he picked them up and put them in. Mrs. Bunny nearly fainted for joy, and when Snip and Snap saw how ill she and Mr. Bunny looked, and heard how much wretchedness and anxiety their escape had caused, they could scarcely eat their breakfast for crying, hungry as they were, and they promised solemnly never to do such a dreadful thing again.

And if the boy had only known this, and known what a deep impression the affair made upon the other six little Bunnies, he would have been saved the trouble of digging another and deeper trench around the rabbit-hutch, and filling it with coal-ashes, and driving down a whole lot of sticks beside the ones already there. But until either people grow clever enough to understand what birds and beasts say, or the birds and beasts learn to talk English and French and ever so many more languages much more difficult than their own, I am afraid there will continue to be misunderstandings and mistakes.

A MAYFLOWER.

UNDERNEATH a pine tree, sheltered
    from the north wind,
  Where the frost repented and melted
    into dew,
And the south wind murmured hopes
    about the summer,
  Which was surely coming, a little
    Mayflower grew.

All the wood was silent, for the trees
    were listening
  For the south wind's whisper that the
    time had come
When the baby-leaves they held, sheathed from frost so safely,
  Might dance out to the music of the wild bee's hum.

But the Mayflower ventured long before the leaves might,
  For she had an errand, and she knew not fear;
Stooping from the treetops to the ground, the south wind
  Told to her a secret which the tall trees did not hear.

Hardly had the last bud opened to the sun's kiss
    When a shout of rapture broke the silence of the wood:
" Here it is, the first one, and a perfect beauty!
    Oh, I *meant* to find one—I was sure I could."

Eagerly but tenderly slender fingers clasped her,
    While the pine tree murmured, mournfully and low,
" Do not leave me, darling; you will only wither.—
    Little child, dear little child, please to let her go "

But the little maiden gently plucked the flower,
    Only saying to herself, " How the pine trees sigh!"
While the Mayflower whispered, " Mother, Mother Pine Tree,
    Trust me with her; I am not afraid of her. Good-bye."

Then the little flower, feeling strangely drowsy,
    Fell asleep in peaceful faith that naught would go amiss:
Nothing more she knew until, to a burst of music,
    Suddenly she wakened, thrilling through with bliss.

Rose triumphant anthems to the King of heaven
    From the white-robed singers and the organ's voice.
" Was not this worth dying for?" thought the little flower.
    " Was I worthy, then, of this? Oh, my heart, rejoice!"

"NOTHING MORE SHE KNEW UNTIL, TO A BURST OF MUSIC."

See Page 252

Faint she grew and fainter, fading with the daylight,
  Heeding not the faintness in her ecstasy divine.
"Better, oh far better," with her dying breath she murmured,
  "One short hour of *this* to me than days beneath the pine.

"Better loving service than all peace and pleasure
  Where the south wind wanders and the sunbeams shine,
Though my life had lasted to its fullest measure,
  It had never reached to this underneath the pine."

AN OLD-FASHIONED FATHER.

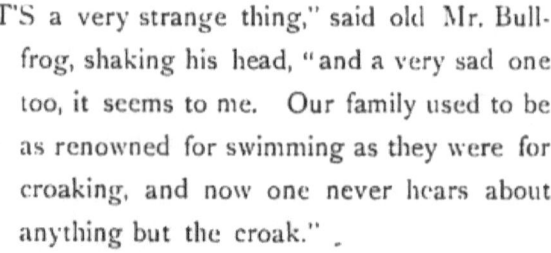

"IT'S a very strange thing," said old Mr. Bullfrog, shaking his head, "and a very sad one too, it seems to me. Our family used to be as renowned for swimming as they were for croaking, and now one never hears about anything but the croak."

"Can *you* swim, father?" asked little Hop in a subdued voice and manner.

Old Mr. Bullfrog swelled himself up. "I could swim perfectly when I was your age, my son," he answered, "and I still remember the theory quite well enough to teach it. · If your mother will excuse us for an hour or two this evening, you and Skip shall come with me a little way up the bank, where the water is deep, and I will give you a lesson."

So Mrs. Bullfrog gave them an early tea, and soon after Mr. Bullfrog and Hop and Skip found a nice place where the bank went off suddenly; and there Mr. Bullfrog sat down and gave them a lecture on swimming. His instructions were delightfully clear and simple.

"First you jump in," he said. Hop and Skip shuddered.

MR. BULLFROG TEACHING HIS YOUNGSTERS TO SWIM

"Then you draw up your hind legs, like this," he continued, "and shoot them out suddenly, like that. Well, why don't you do it?" he asked impatiently.

Hop and Skip immediately did it, all but the jumping in.

"You can't swim on dry land," said their father. "Why don't you jump in?"

"It makes me feel all gone here, just to think of it," said Hop, putting his hand on his stomach, and little Skip shrank back from the edge in terror.

"Now, this is all nonsense," said Mr. Bullfrog angrily. "If you'll just do as I *say*, and not as I *do*, you'll have no trouble at all. I could swim like a duck when I was no older than Skip.—You ought to set your little brother a better example, Hop."

"If you'd just *show* us once, father," said Hop meekly, "I think we could do it: we'd see then that it could be done."

Mr. Bullfrog sat on the bank and thought for at least five minutes. And while he was thinking he remembered that when *his* father taught him things he said "Come" much oftener than he said "Go," so that when he did say "Go," Mr. Bullfrog had hastened to mind him.

"Come, children," said Mr. Bullfrog pleasantly; and, jumping up as he spoke, he "took a header" from the bank, and came up smiling, though he was puffing and blowing too, while Hop and Skip looked on in terror. Mr. Bullfrog reached up, caught Hop's leg, and pulled him into the water; then he turned and swam gracefully backward, saying, "Come on now—swim toward me; you'll not sink, and if you do I'll catch you."

And Hop, when he recovered from his first scare, found that he could swim quite well, and enjoyed it.

"You'll not do *me* that way, will you, father?" implored little Skip from the bank as Mr. Bullfrog floated upon his back.

"Not if you'll jump in without it, my son," said Mr. Bullfrog encouragingly. "Just look how Hop's enjoying himself out there beyond the cat-tails. Come—one! *two*! THREE!" At "THREE" Skip actually did plunge in, and in a few minutes was swimming gayly about with his brother and father.

"Why, you're all wet, father! did you go in too?" asked Mrs. Bullfrog when the party, in great spirits, returned home about an hour later.

"Yes, I went in too, mother," said Mr. Bullfrog, smiling; "and I'll get you just to rub me down with a burdock-leaf if you're not too tired: I don't care about having rheumatism if I can help it, but I found that it's much easier to teach swimming in water than on land."

A HOT SUPPER.

IT was the first moth of the season, and a very large one. Five young sparrows all saw it at once, and each made a dart for it, but the moth had no idea of being eaten by one sparrow, not to speak of five; so he fluttered off as fast as his rather weak wings could carry him, and then began a hot pursuit. The five sparrows hustled along, beating each other with their wings, making rude speeches, nipping each other's toes, each one struggling to be first in the race. Of course, in a struggle like this nobody could get on very fast, and the moth, who had been greatly terrified at first, began to laugh to himself as he found how easily he could keep ahead of them all.

"I'll just lead them a dance," he said, "quarrelsome little wretches! It's lucky for me it isn't Cock Robin's family, where they always go by ages, or Jenny Wren's, where the one who can catch anything divides it with the rest. It's a pretty long stretch to the belfry, but I think I can manage it: my wings feel stronger than they did when I started, and when I get there I can slip in between the slats, where they can't possibly follow."

And, chuckling to himself as he thought how angry and disappointed the sparrows would be, he flew lightly on, sometimes pausing a moment until all five thought they were sure of him, and then flying rapidly to make the chase a little more exciting for them, until he gained the belfry without over-fatiguing himself in the least. He poised himself a moment on a twig of ivy, and then, just as the whole five made a sort of hustling rush for him at once, crawled between two slats, and peeped out to see five foolish-looking sparrows, very much out of breath with the long chase and the bump which they had given themselves against the belfry, turn sullenly about and begin to fly wearily home.

"Which of you caught it, my dears?" asked Cock Robin pleasantly as the five dropped heavily down on a branch near his door. He had seen the beginning of the chase, but not the end.

"We didn't any of us catch it." said the oldest sparrow angrily. "*I'd* have caught it half a dozen times if the rest would have kept back and given me half a chance; but they all pushed and crowded so that the moth got away—selfish, greedy things! It was the first moth of the season too, and as fat as butter!"

"I suppose," said Cock Robin quietly, "that any one of you could have caught it half a dozen times if the rest had kept back and given him half a chance. We can't all be first in the race,

"FIVE YOUNG SPARROWS SAW IT, AND EACH MADE A DART FOR IT."

See Page 261.

you know, but there's a certain pleasure in being second or third or fourth, or even fifth, if somebody we love is first." And, pouncing on a large worm which was engaged in measuring the tree upon which they were sitting, Cock Robin said "Good-evening" as well as he could with his mouth full, and took the worm to his family

The five little sparrows looked at each other. They felt very much ashamed as well as very hungry.

"I'm sorry," said the oldest sparrow softly, and he nestled up to the next one.

"I'm sorry too," said the next; and so it went on until all five had said it, and were sitting so close together on the bough that they looked liked one large sparrow with five small heads.

Perhaps you think that they meant they were sorry because the moth got away? No doubt they were sorry for that, for it was too late now to catch anything, and they were obliged to go to bed without any supper. But, somehow, I do not think that that was exactly what they meant, and Cock Robin, who is a very observing bird, does not think so either.

ONE STEP AT A TIME.

WE had walked so far since morning,
    For you see we were too poor
To hire a cart to take us
    Across the lonely moor.
We had all been down with the fever;
    Mother and father were gone,
And grandmother said, "My Gertrude,
    We must make our way to John.

"We will sell the little left us;
    It will keep us till we get
Some work to do in the village;
    I can do a day's work yet.
And John has room in his cottage
    To give us a corner there,
And he and his wife will welcome us,
    Though it's little they have to spare."

We seemed to get no farther,
    Though we had walked quite fast,

"SHE TURNED ASIDE TO A FURZE-BANK, AND WEARILY SANK DOWN."

See Page 289.

Till I saw the village-steeple,
   In the distance still, at last.
But just as I said, " Dear grandma,
   Look, yonder is the town!"
She turned aside to a furze-bank,
   And wearily sank down.

" I can go no farther, darling,"
   She said to me with a groan ;
" Leave me here, my little Gertrude,
   And go you on alone.
I am not afraid to stay here ;
   Nothing will do me harm ;
And maybe John will come for me :
   I could walk with his stout young arm."

But I was not going to leave her.
   " Oh, grandma dear," I said,
" Just look how near the town is,
   And the road lies straight ahead.
It can't be far, for, listen,
   We can hear the church-bells chime ;
Come, lean on me and take one step—
   Just one step at a time."

She tottered on, I leading,
    And as the sun went down
We reached the little cottage:
    It is just outside the town.
How uncle and aunt did kiss us!
    What welcoming words they said!
There never was such a supper
    Or such a lovely bed.

"HE PIPES FOR MY DOLLY'S DANCING."

Now we are at home and happy;
    The troubled times are gone;
I spell and knit with grandma,
    And play with little John.

He pipes for my dolly's dancing,
    And we sing to her this rhyme:
"Dance high, dance low, wherever you go,
    You'll always have to take, you know,
        Just one step at a time."

And when the little children
    Who go with us to school
Say they cannot learn their lessons
    Or they cannot keep a rule,
I tell them about our journey,
    And say, "To walk or climb,
To study or work, or even play,
    It's one step at a time."

"I TELL THEM ABOUT OUR JOURNEY."

THE THREE B'S.

THEIR mother called them her three B's, because their names were Betty and Bell and Bob; but they were not always busy bees, by any means. They lived in a small house near the seashore, and they could spend whole mornings making sand-forts and houses and hunting shells and seaweed, but it made their backs ache dreadfully to do a little weeding in the garden, and they groaned regularly every morning when school-time came. And they were always a great deal more interested in what was for dinner, and when it would be Saturday, than they were in their lessons.

They were playing on the beach one day when a pleasant-faced lady with pretty brown eyes and a kind smile sat down near them and began to make a sketch of the sea, and an old boat which had been hauled up to be mended, and some nets which had been stretched out to dry. She talked to them as she drew, and showed them her sketch when it was done; and Betty, after gazing at it in silent astonishment for a few minutes, exclaimed, "Can you make pictures of cows, ma'am, as well as of boats and nets?"

"Not quite so well," replied the lady, smiling, "for cows are

"THEY WOULD SPEND WHOLE MORNINGS MAKING SAND-FORTS."

more difficult to draw than boats and nets are; but why do you ask?"

"Because I thought you might like to take the likeness of our Jet and Pearl, and the white calf that hasn't any name yet; it's like a story, and it would make such a pretty picture."

"And what is the story?" asked the lady.

"They each had a calf, ma'am," said Bell, thinking it was her turn, "and Jet's calf died. Father took it away in the night, and the next morning each one seemed to think that the calf that was left was hers. They did not fight about it, but one seems just as fond of it as the other does, and it does not seem to know which is its mother."

"I should like very much to make a sketch of such a remarkable family," said the lady, "and if I succeed in finding board in the neighborhood perhaps I can. Do you know of any one who could take me?"

"I do believe mother would," said Betty eagerly. "Her spareroom's empty, and I heard her say a day or two ago that she'd like a quiet boarder for a few weeks this summer."

"I am very quiet indeed," said the lady, laughing; "so if you will show me the way, we will go and ask her. I shall be out sketching nearly all day, and she will not find me troublesome."

Mrs. Ferguson was very glad to let her room to the pleasant-looking lady, who introduced herself as Miss Clayton, and who was so easily satisfied about her accommodations that Mrs. Ferguson said she "wished all boarders were like her."

The children called her "our boarder," and took a lively interest in all her sketches and pictures.

A rainy day came after she had been with them about a week —not rainy enough, the children's mother assured them, to keep them from school, but quite too wet for out-of-doors painting.

JET AND PEARL AND THE CALF.

"BOB DREW A BRUSHFUL OF GREEN PAINT ACROSS THE PICTURE."

Miss Clayton, however, had discovered a very pretty view from the half-open pump-shed; so here, with Mrs. Ferguson's permission, she established herself and went to work. Her sketch was nearly finished when, the rain having ceased, she went up stairs to open her windows, and while she was gone the three B's appeared on the scene.

For a few minutes they looked at the picture from a respectful distance; then they gradually drew nearer, and at last Bob took up the brush, saying, "It don't look hard when she does it.. I mean to fix this hill; she hasn't it near green enough."

They were so completely absorbed, Bob in "fixing" the hill and Betty and Bell in breathlessly watching him, that they did not hear Miss Clayton's step until she was close upon them, and then Bob, in his consternation, drew the brushful of green paint across nearly the whole picture.

Miss Clayton's face was no longer pleasant as she gathered up her drawing-materials and with the ruined sketch in her hand went straight to Mrs. Ferguson.

"I am very sorry," she said, "but it will be impossible for me to remain here any longer, Mrs. Ferguson. As it happens, this sketch is of little consequence, but your children might destroy more valuable work and more valuable materials. I can have no confidence in them after this. I will pay my board to the end of the week, but I shall leave you this afternoon." And Miss Clayton went to her room to pack her trunks.

I don't believe any of the many little children who think they must touch things to see them, and who meddle just because they like meddling, ever felt worse about the consequences of their bad behavior than these three little Fergusons did. Their mother lost "the best boarder she ever had," and they lost a pleasant friend, but they gained something out of this sad experience: they learned a lesson which they did not forget. When Bob had told his mother all about it, she wished to explain to Miss Clayton that Betty and Bell had taken no active part in the mischief, but they begged her not to, for "If we'd asked Bob to let the picture alone, he'd have done it," said Betty—"now, wouldn't you, Bob?"

And Bob, after thinking a minute, said reluctantly "Well, yes, I believe I would."

"I've just one thing to say," said Mrs. Ferguson when Miss Clayton had gone, "and then we'll let bygones be bygones: you like me to call you my three B's, but if you don't leave the army of hinderers and join the army of helpers before long, I shall call you my three wasps."

MAKING A TABLEAU.

DID you ever help make a tableau?
  I don't believe you did;
And you needn't want to, either:
  it's the worst thing in the world.
You're dressed in foolish old fixings,
  and twisted and turned and chid,
And it's very nearly the death of
  you, just having your back hair
  curled.

We were feeding Pug and her puppies; I was standing on the mat,
  And Nurse was there with Baby, and mamma was at her lunch,
When Aunt Alice came in and said to mamma, "Now, Mary, look
  at that!
  She's the one for the Reynolds picture;" and she looked as
  pleased as Punch.

Mamma just laughed a little, and said, "Try it if you will;
  She does look like the picture, but you'll have to curl her hair,
And you'll have to find a recipe for making her keep still.
  But if you wish to, do it by all means—*I* don't care."

"AUNT ALICE STOOD ME ON A CHAIR BEFORE A LITTLE GIRL."

See Page 283

So she took me off to try it, and I was pleased at first;
I thought it must be splendid to stand in a large gilt frame.

"WE WERE FEEDING PUG AND HER PUPPIES."

You see, I was so little that I didn't know the worst,
But I found it out, I tell you, when that dreadful evening came!

Aunt Alice stood me on a chair before a little girl
In a stupid painted picture, and dressed me up like that;

And she said, "Now, Bertie, *do not* let your hair get out of curl:
   If the pictures don't go off well, the whole thing will be flat."

If we'd only had the pictures first, and after that the fun,
   Perhaps I'd not have minded, or not so much; but, oh,
They kept the pictures for the last, when everything was done,
   And every single thing I tried to do they nagged me so.

They stopped me in the middle of a game of Blindman's Buff.
   The very boy who was to help to make the picture said,
"Don't let us play this, Bertie—it's very much too rough;
   There won't be time to fix it if you should spoil your head."

They had let me take the cap off, because it looked so queer,
   And the gown, because it tripped me and nearly made me fall;
But Aunt Alice said, "I'll call you when it's time to dress you, dear,
   And, whatever you are doing, come the minute that I call."

Now, only just to think of it! I heard Aunt Alice scream—
   Yes, she *did* scream too—"Come, Bertie!" and of course I had to go,
When I'd just been helped that minute to strawberries and cream:
   Yes, I'd like to see Aunt Alice if mamma should treat *her* so.

"THEY STOPPED ME IN THE MIDDLE OF A GAME OF BLINDMAN'S BUFF."

See Page 284.

I didn't care for anything : I tell you I was mad ;
　But I let her put the things on me, and stepped into the frame ;
The people clapped, and some one said, " Her little face is sad.
　It's a very lovely picture. What is the dear child's name?"

It was not worth the strawberries, just being called " dear child,"
　And I did not at all wonder that my little face was sad :
They kept me standing still there till I thought I should go wild,
　And they never saved my strawberries : now, was not that too bad?

A YOUNG EGYPTIAN.

WHAT a very solemn-looking little boy! He does not look as if he had ever run or shouted, or really played, in all his life. Perhaps the strange solemnity of the land in which he lives, with its wonderful river Nile, which until quite lately hid its source from explorers, its great frowning Pyramids, its huge head of the Sphinx, makes even the little children look as if the weight of hundreds of years was upon them. Even the great birds which frequent the Nile have the same solemn look—serious-looking pelicans and cranes, beautiful white herons and ducks. And, before the steamboats came to frighten them away, crocodiles showed their ugly heads in the river.

Perhaps you will think that this little Egyptian's solemn face is accounted for by the fact that there is no winter in Egypt, and that he can never go coasting or sliding or skating, or have a good game of snowballing or help to make a snow-man. For there are but two seasons in his land, spring and summer, and the latter lasts from April to November. But if little steamboats keep on fuss-

"WHAT A VERY SOLEMN-LOOKING LITTLE BOY!"

ing up and down the Nile, and inquisitive travellers go poking about among the Pyramids and ruins, it will not be long before the solemn ways of the Egyptians begin to grow brisk and business-like, and instead of behaving as if they had "all the time there is," they may begin to act as the rest of the world does, which is very much like the famous

"Old woman of Surrey,
Who was morn, noon, and night in a hurry."

UNCLE MOSES.

I'M always very glad indeed when market-day
comes round :
A better story-teller than old Moses can't be
found.
We call him Uncle Moses, for he's very fond of
boys ;
He is always glad to see us, and he does not mind our noise.

He sits all day in market with a pile of queer old things,
And when he is not talking he smokes his pipe and sings ;
And he tells us made-up stories in such a funny way
We would always, for the sake of one, leave any sort of play.

They all begin " I dreamed one night—" and I'll just tell you
one
He told me when I said I wished that I might have a gun.
" What for?" asked Uncle Moses.—" To shoot birds and things,"
said I.—
" So," said he, " it makes you happy to see little creatures die ?

"I used to go out shooting, and I thought it a great feat
 When I'd bring a lot of things home that I didn't want to eat;
 But I thought a little different after what I dreamed one night:
 I saw the other side of it, and nearly died of fright.

"SO ONE HE PICKS MY DOG UP, AND ANOTHER PICKS UP ME."

"Six great big black bears caught me out hunting with my dog,
 And one of them he braced himself against a heavy log,
 And he says to all the others, 'Now, if you want some fun,
 Just hold them both quite steady while I shoot them with their gun.'

"WHEN HE IS NOT SMOKING, HE TELLS MADE-UP STORIES."

See Page 291.

"So one he picks my dog up, and another picks up me,
And two of them 'most laugh themselves to death against a tree ;
And an ugly little fellow, with his hair all in a mat,
Says, 'Fair play is a jewel! Look here, I'll hold his hat!'

"My dog he howled like forty, and I gave such a scream
That I woke right up. My goodness! that was an awful dream!
And if the things feel that way when we shoot them, don't you
    see,
If we do not need to eat them we'd better let them be."

A GENEROUS DOG.

BOUNCE was the big dog, and Dot was the little one. Bounce had always lived at Mr. Barry's; he could remember no other home, and Reginald and Florence, who were both younger than Bounce, had loved him ever since they were babies. He was a great black Newfoundland, with large, kind eyes, and a bark that sounded like distant thunder; and not so very distant, either. He loved both the children devotedly, but he seemed to think that Florence was less able to take care of herself than Reginald was to take care of himself; and whenever he had to choose between them, he always elected to go with Florence. Their home was a large, pleasant country-house within a mile of the sea, and it was a favorite amusement to take Bounce to the beach and send him into the water after sticks. He was a famous swimmer and not at all afraid of the breakers, and he would dash into them as often as the children chose to throw a stick. He had never had a rival, for he considered it quite beneath his dignity to be jealous of cats and chickens and rabbits and guinea-pigs, and nobody had ever thought of such a thing as wanting another dog while they had Bounce.

But when Mr. and Mrs. Barry and Florence and Reginald came home from a long drive one summer evening, they found a little puppy lying on the door-mat. He was so extremely small that they very nearly stepped on him before they saw him, and instead of being frightened and running away, he got up and welcomed them as if he had known them all his life and had been anxiously waiting for them to come home. He was a little black-and-tan terrier, and Jake, the man-of-all-work, who was an authority on the subject of dogs, said very positively that he would grow but little larger than his present size. The children were much delighted with this, and easily persuaded their father and mother to let them keep the little waif, who had evidently been a much-petted dog. Inquiry was made in the neighborhood for his owner, but no one knew anything about him. The only clue to his sudden appearance was the fact that a strange carriage had been seen driving along the beach upon the afternoon of his sudden appearance upon Mr. Barry's door-mat. Mr. Barry wrote a notice of his finding, giving a full description of him and telling where his present home was: this he tacked up in the post-office, and for several days the children were in hourly dread of the appearance of his owner. But when a week had passed and no one had come to claim him, they decided that all danger was over and that they might consider him their own. They had "tried" various names on him, and they imagined that he had showed signs of recognition when they called him "Dot;" so they had chosen this for his name; and, whether or not he had ever owned it before, he soon knew it, and answered to it in a very satisfactory manner.

At first Bounce had taken very little notice of Dot: he evidently regarded him as a "transient" and quite beneath the notice of a "permanent." But when he gradually discovered that the stranger was being made one of the family, his indignation rose. He had been first and only dog too long to find any pleasure in sharing his rights and privileges, and as Dot's manner became more assured, and he behaved more and more as if he felt entirely at home, and considered himself as of a good deal of consequence, Bounce grew surlier, and from letting Dot severely alone he began to growl, and even to snap, at him. The children were both surprised and grieved. They tried to convince Bounce that they were not taking any of the love which had always belonged to him to bestow upon the little stranger, but Bounce either could not or would not understand. He would not permit Dot to eat anywhere near his kennel and dish, and once, when Dot ventured to help himself to some of the dinner which Bounce had left, Bounce gave such a savage and menacing growl that the little dog fled under the porch in terror, and would not be coaxed out for a long time.

Bounce had an amiable weakness for crackers, and was always ready to "speak" and give his paw to be shaken, and even make clumsy efforts to stand on his hind legs, at the mere mention of the word. To the great amusement of the children, Dot, without any teaching, began to copy's all Bounce's tricks, and, being so much smaller and lighter, soon succeeded in performing them better than his pattern could. It was touching to see the little fellow's humble admiration for the great dog, and his timid offers of friendship. He was rebuffed again and again, but he always seemed, when he met Bounce the next time, to be hoping that since their last encounter Bounce might have seen reasons for changing his mind, until at last Florence told him that he had "no proper pride," and that he ought to wait until Bounce begged his pardon before he made any further attempts at friendship.

Bounce was as friendly and affectionate as ever to every one else, and his spirits always rose when they went to the beach, for here he was supreme. Dot was evidently afraid of the water, and no amount of coaxing could prevail upon him to go in. And not only was he afraid to venture himself, but he always gave a howl of alarm whenever he saw Bounce plunge into the breakers, and rushed up and down the beach in great excitement and anxiety until he saw him come out again.

"If we could only get Dot to go in once," said Reginald one day as he and Florence sat on the rocks watching Bounce swim fearlessly in after a stick. "I don't believe he would be afraid any more.

'It is the first step that costs.' You know how afraid you were, Flo, the first time we went in bathing, and how soon you got over it. I've a great mind to throw Dot in a little way, just enough to wet him all over, and after he has found that it doesn't kill him he will probably go in himself."

"I don't know," said Florence doubtfully. "He's so very little that I don't wonder the waves look so frightfully large to him; and you know when he's badly frightened he just drops on his back and holds up all his paws; and if he were to do that he would be swept right out to sea."

"Oh, I should not put him far enough in for that," replied Reginald. "I mean to try it, anyhow: he loses so much fun by not learning to swim, and Bounce crows over him so about it."

"Well, don't put him in far," said Florence, following Reginald over the rocks until they were as close to the edge of the sea as they could go without being touched by the waves.

Dot was a confiding little dog, and, not suspecting what was in store for him, had been caught without any trouble, and now Reginald gave him a gentle throw into a retreating wave, saying as he did so, "If he doesn't like it he can just scramble out, you know."

But it happened as Florence had feared: the little dog, very much frightened, fell helplessly on his back, and a great wave swept him away before Reginald could catch him. Bounce had come out, and was standing on the rocks, but as Dot disappeared he plunged in, and almost before the children had time to be frightened came out again with his small rival in his mouth. Dot lay still for a few minutes as if stunned, and the big dog, evidently thinking him dead, gave a dismal howl and began licking the little

"REGINALD GAVE DOT A GENTLE THROW INTO A WAVE."

one's face. Dot "came to" almost immediately, and was soon frisking about as if nothing had happened, but, to the surprise of the children, Bounce no longer regarded him as an enemy; and they thought it quite as curious that Dot seemed, immediately and entirely, to understand the change in Bounce's views. They ate out of the same dish; Dot marched boldly into Bounce's kennel, and, under the protection of his big friend, soon ventured into the water and forgot his fears. Bounce's friendliness was as great as his enmity had been, and the two dogs became almost inseparable.

"And the moral of that is," said Florence one day when she and Reginald were discussing the change in Bounce's views, "that if we don't like anybody we'd better go to work and try to do something for him, and see if that will not make us like him."

THE END.